ALAN BOOTH

Christian Nonconformity in International Affairs

London EPWORTH PRESS

Printed in 10/12pt Times
by The Garden City Press Limited
Letchworth, Hertfordshire

SBN 7162 0148 8

*Christian Nonconformity
in International Affairs*

The Beckly Social Service Lecture 1970

Contents

1 Ecclesiastical Explosion

In 1946, for the first time in human history, Christian churches set up an official common instrument to work for peace on a universal scale.

In 1963 Pope John issued his encyclical 'Pacem in Terris' and the Second Vatican Council thereafter plunged into a historic debate on the whole subject.

The great argument about what Christians and churches should be doing in the field of international affairs has thus exploded, and all sorts of traditional assumptions have been blown up with it. It is probable that few people are fully aware of the range and extent of the task of construction ahead of us, if we are to realize anything of our visions of ecumenical Christian service in the building of a humane and just world community.

This book is an attempt to sketch out the jobs ahead and indicate from my own experience what I believe are the fruitful lines of advance.

But first let us look at this explosion to see if it is really true that we are facing a novel and historically unprecedented situation.

The first and obvious novelty is that in the last 150 years 'for the first time in its history Christianity made actual its inherent genius and became world-wide. In this it surpassed the achievement of every other religion' (Professor Kenneth Latourette in his *The Expansion of Christianity*).

Instead of seeing themselves as partners in the 'civilizing mission' of European nations to the rest of the world, Christians have recently tried to grasp a new image of themselves as representatives of the human race as such. So for the first time they find themselves in business on a truly international scale. The absorbing quarrels of

Europe no longer obsess them so exclusively. The age-old confrontation with Islam, fought to a standstill in the Middle East, Eastern Europe, North Africa and the shores of Spain, no longer seems to set the geographical limits of 'Christendom'.

The missionary movement of the last centuries has jumped over all these barriers, and has left us with a Christian community trying to strike its own roots in many cultures and civilizations. So it is also an ecumenical community which feels for the first time the real strains of human divergences and differences. The neat and tidy intellectual systems we have inherited from the scholars of Europe about what the rôle of churches may be in supra-national affairs no longer fit our situation. We must start again.

Then, of course, it has been difficult, to put it mildly, for churches to find a very convincing rôle in international construction while they were busy fighting each other. There are easy taunts and essays in moral superiority available by the gross to those who want to ridicule churches and Christian communities suddenly grown respectable and conciliatory after centuries of contributing a fierce intransigence and brutality to the conflicts of nations. If it gives anyone comfort now to repent of the European wars of religion, no doubt he must be allowed to indulge his taste though he would probably be better employed in finding penitent means of deflecting the mounting violence of our own century. But we can all agree that the contemporary realization, so far as it has gone, of Christian ecumenical fellowship has opened a new possibility that Christians might be more useful in the future in helping men to avoid mutual destruction.

It is not simply that Christians are learning to respect each other. Something deeper has occurred, which affects the relations of Christians, not only to each other, but to people of other persuasions altogether. It is the discovery of the Christian gospel as the possession and treasure of the human race as a whole, to be understood the more profoundly as many different cultures and traditions delve into its truth. Obviously these new insights are not common coin amongst Christians. It is the pioneering adventurers of the spirit who are responsible for calling attention to them. But then it is precisely these creative originators who in fact determine the future shape of events.

The third novelty is a result of the other two. It is that we can no longer see clearly what are the proper relations of the Christian community, and their institutional church organizations, to the structures of political power in the world. The patterns worked out so cosily or so arduously in the domestic history of Europe are now intolerably archaic. Popes and emperors, archbishops and monarchs and parliaments, even the institutionalized radicalism of the free church tradition, do not export well to Asia or Africa. They belong to a corner of the world, and a corner of human history, which we can soberly respect without having to believe it to be normative for other periods or other continents.

But as soon as we confess confusion about the relation of Christians and their churches to the structures of political power in the world, we admit that we are at a loss about how to be effective in the cause of international justice and peace. The two questions are inescapably linked. And until we find some sort of new answer to the first we shall be completely at odds with each other about how to deal with practical day-to-day choices of action in the political field. If, for instance, the proper stance of the Christians and their churches is as perpetual critics of those who exercise political power, then, at any time of mounting crisis or crushing oppression, their task is clear.

If, on the other hand, there was some validity in the old notion that Christians and their churches had some share of responsibility for the ordering of public life, however well or badly they discharged it, then at such times their course of action will tend to be quite different. If, perhaps, there is a third way in between, whereby Christians take seriously their Lord's example of abjuring all claim to political power, while accepting a great responsibility for human destiny, then some very new rôles will have to be thought out to take account of this double obligation. But, whatever course is chosen, one thing is certain—it will be new at least in the sense that it will necessarily have to be thought out all over again, from the bottom up.

No wonder, therefore, that we are floundering in the waves of new experience. After all, the events we are talking about occurred only in recent decades; yesterday afternoon, in terms of church history. It is not surprising that many of the arguments hotly being pursued today still proceed with presuppositions and terminology derived from very different earlier times. The argument about revolution versus *status quo* is a marvellous anachronism in a world in which many would not recognize a *status quo* if they saw one, simply because none has existed in their lifetime. Much of the debate between pacifism and non-pacifism belongs to the domestic fireside discussion of a 'Christendom' long since evaporated and is likely to take insufficient account of the minority status of Christians on the world scale, and, on the other hand, of their new sense of responsibility in universal terms.

Linked with all this, is our struggle to rethink what it is we refer to as the Christian Church. It made life so much simpler when so many Christians thought of the Church as expressing itself chiefly by pronouncements of Popes and Archbishops, or their energetic exercise of influence with those in authority. But once we all take seriously what many free churches have long maintained (at least in theory) that the church is a community, the significant members of which are in the vast majority laymen, then we are in real trouble. Laymen do not like the tendency of prelates to pronounce, as though from some theological mountain top, on questions they manifestly do not fully understand. Worse still, laymen are not normally given to 'pronouncing' much at all. Their daily lives are less conditioned by pulpit experience than by the effort to make an awkward sort of world work reasonably well for another year or two. The two styles of life make for very different preoccupations when it comes to thinking what is the best thing to be done next in international construction.

Perhaps the contrast of lay and clerical here is not completely fair. It may be that the real distinction is between the didactic and the practical type of human being, with the suggestion that the rôle of the clergy tends to put them in the didactic category. But, if so, they have plenty of interesting company. Much of the intellectual community will be there too. Indeed, perhaps as we press on into the bewildering future, one of the most dangerous failures of understanding will be between those who get 'stuck in' to manipulating as best they can the system as they inherited it, learning the skills and devices which make it possible to steer it roughly in a tolerable direction; and those so appalled by its potentialities that they withdraw into the rather unrewarding activity of being negative commentators. If that happens, we must see that neither group claims that it is 'the church'. Rather we must struggle on, trying to hold both within the one argumentative family. The temptation will be to hand over the church to the professors and the commentators. For these are the people most likely to have time to attend ecclesiastical committees and conferences, and most articulate in philosophical debate—the sort of people who are a godsend to lonely clergy even if they sometimes seem 'a pain in the neck' to people trying to make 'the system' work.

When it comes to international affairs nothing may be more important than the insistence that neither type has a pre-eminent theological validity, and that both are needed if we are to find the way ahead. This will be the acid test as to whether we mean real business about the church as a lay community.

As if all that was not a sufficient agenda, there is still one more novelty which may prove the most troublesome of all. It is referred to in professional theological circles as the emphasis on secularity. One of the most heartening developments of these days has been the discovery, for which some of us have long hoped and prayed, that the world is to be loved, not shunned, by Christians and indeed that they are supposed to regard themselves primarily as members of the human race rather than as either the world's mentors or its judges. What men are concerned about is thereby our concern. What they aspire to achieve is thereby our business. The 'secular' world is not over against the 'sacred' but is the place where sacredness is and can be manifested. We have at last accepted the invitation to join the human race and identify ourselves with its fate even as God did in the incarnation and the crucifixion—only it has taken us rather a long time to get the message.

But this presents us at once with a new dilemma. Is it the first duty of the Christian community to identify itself unreservedly with all those human causes and movements aspiring to promote a wider justice and freedom amongst men? Should we in our new found humility see our function in the international community as lending our modest support to programmes and policies others have devised for the common good as they apprehend it? Strong forces are at work to define our job in such terms. Thereby we certainly gain in popularity in an age which finds our dogmatic and peculiar characteristics quite alien, yet is not so harsh as to wish for our total liquidation. We are offered a rôle in society of being the great suppliers of unearthly backing for fashionable policies.

The alternative seems to call in question our new respect for secularity. It is the harder road of being at once the fundamental lover and the fundamental critic of the world. As a propaganda line it simply cannot compete with the first position. It is awkward, independent, unfashionable, non-conformist. It has the disadvantage of a certain lack of simplicity, which makes it hard to put over on the mass media. To feel strongly in good company is much more agreeable than to think alone. No wonder as Christians we shrink from such a calling. But we cannot escape the issue. It can be put in the following way.

Churches have for centuries given the impression of wanting to distinguish themselves from the rest of the world, of wanting to teach, uplift, improve, correct but never completely identify. No doubt at every period they have produced the servants of the poor and needy who personally blazed the trail of identification for all mankind. But as institutions the churches take credit for producing these saints while seeming anxious to justify a self-regarding emphasis on separateness and special privilege for themselves.

Now the trend is happily in another direction. With their wealth and prestige much depleted, their rôle in society diminished and confused, they seem to be in search of a function which will make them the champions of the great inarticulate and dispossessed multitude of mankind. Instead of separateness they emphasize belonging, for privilege they at least speak of substituting involvement. And so they raise the question whether they can bring to the forum of the world's affairs anything to refresh the discussion and abate the frustration more than a 'me too' alignment with the cries of the helpless. Are they going to be just the supernatural embellishment of whatever populist movement happens to be in vogue? Or have they a more peculiar and distinctive task to fulfil, which brings new life and also new persecution? Somehow the tenor of the New Testament suggests the latter as the more likely possibility. But it is one which the churches are spiritually unprepared for, in their longing to commend themselves to their day and age.

This survey of the landscape to be explored would be seriously incomplete if we failed to identify who the explorers are. The Methodist Church has a long tradition of concern for peace and justice in the world. But now it finds itself only a small part of a great company. We are used to working with our British colleagues, Anglican, Baptist, Congregationalist, Presbyterian and Quaker. It is always a shock to discover that they are easier to get on with than members of our own denomination rooted in another part of the world—particularly on public issues. Now, however, we have awoken to the fact that we have to throw our contribution into a common pool where it is small enough alongside the great traditions of continental Protestantism, Eastern Orthodoxy and the characteristic originality of North America.

But all of this may prove simple and easy going compared with the really exciting novelty of our day—the prospect of co-operation in this task between the churches in membership of the World Council of Churches and the Roman Catholic Church. We are only at the beginning of exploration in this field. What it will mean for us all is not clear. But it adds greatly to the challenge to each one of us to try to think out what in our view the churches should be doing to fulfil faithfully their assignment in the building of a world community. For only by tidying up our own muddles can we be constructive partners with our fellow Christians struggling with the historical muddles of their own traditions.

2 Can We Influence Decisions?

'I have before me the current issue of the *New Christian* in which the General Secretary of the British Council of Churches, Dr. Kenneth Sansbury, reported on the Crete meeting of the Central Committee of the World Council of Churches. One paragraph runs as follows: "The Central Committee reiterated what it had already said about Viet Nam, called for full religious liberty in Spain and offered the services of a mediator in Nigeria. It expressed serious concern over the world's food gap and protested against racial discrimination." It is little wonder that the Church has almost ceased to be the target of satirical comedians. Not even the sharpest wit amongst them can parody us as effectively as we parody ourselves. But the image conjured up by that extraordinary paragraph ought to have been worth five minutes of the "Frost Report"—this august body of men, trotting metaphorically round the world expressing concern at this, grave concern at that and very grave concern at something else.'[1]

This makes an admirable starting point for me, for was I not professionally involved in the very case in point? And it fixes attention at the outset on the danger of imagining that a statement is in some way a courageous and effective sort of activity. Archbishop William Temple used to complain that when people said 'the church should do something' they really meant 'the Archbishops should say something'. So deeply ingrained is the sermonic obsession. We think of Christian witness mainly in verbal terms, and of public Christian witness in terms of a manifesto. But the trouble about our words is that they *do* return to us void, having accomplished nothing of what needed to be done. We easily confuse histrionics and sensationalism with daring and courage, when in fact

[1] Colin Morris, *Include me out*, Epworth Press, 1968.

they cost us nothing at all but enhance our reputation as 'interesting and significant'. And I suspect that at the last we shall not be asked 'What attitude did you take?' but more astringently 'What did you do?'

So what is the value of the 'statement' issuing from ecclesiastical sources on current international problems? Its attraction is clear enough. First of all it relieves feelings, and the fact that it is corporately approved gives a sense that it has real punch behind it. The sense, however, is largely illusory, or rather the illusion consists in the belief that the vigorous punch is delivered at a critical spot and is not just a fierce gesture in the empty air. Unfortunately that is exactly what it usually is.

For one thing, anyone who is familiar with the decision-making processes in modern government realizes that they are not noticeably influenced by messages from outside bodies, particularly those which have no clearly defined electoral significance. Someone who can offer a fresh angle, new information, or some particular expertise can, with luck and the right contacts, feed an idea into the process at a particular moment. And of course any body of citizens can address the community at large with the intention of contributing to the formation of public opinion. But the power and weight in both cases depends a great deal on the reputation of the body or person who is uttering, a reputation for competence, seriousness, objectivity and reliability. That is an additional reason for keeping 'statements' to those very few occasions when the churches for some reason are in a particularly fortunate position in the matter of knowledge, competence or objectivity.

Alas, this is not the test usually applied. In practice the decision depends far more on the extent of emotional excitement an issue raises in the community, so that the portentous remark begins to be heard 'We cannot keep silent'. To which the answer ought usually to be 'Why ever not, unless you have something special to say, and some particular authority for saying it?' To keep an ecclesiastical running commentary going on the world's affairs is a sign either of pride or an anxiety neurosis.

There is of course a secondary and hidden objective in the issuing of ecclesiastical statements. It is the sustaining of the ecumenical (or denominational) fellowship itself, the prevention of its flying apart on political issues. By maintaining the illusion that we are addressing governments and peoples with a word of admonition and correction we manage to stage a discussion among ourselves all the freer for appearing to be directed at someone else, and we struggle towards a form of words to represent our view which in reality is the symbol of something quite different. It is the visible testimony to two things. One is that we corporately acknowledge a profound if confused obligation to do something about cruel and destructive conflicts among men. The other is that we do not intend to break up our fellowship even when we fail to agree precisely on political issues.

Our form of words tends to reflect these two concerns pretty accurately—serious in its religious approach, ambiguous and general or very evenly balanced in its political recommendations. Thus we avoid the real nub of most crises—who should act how without waiting for reciprocity? We do, however, do something for ourselves, even at the cost of a little public absurdity, and it may be something we have to do for survival. The trouble is that even a modest absurdity seriously prejudices our reputation, our one asset for real political influence.

Colin Morris, with some qualifications, concludes that 'It is the moral force of our willingness to out-sacrifice everyone else in the field that alone gives us the right to speak. In religion as in roulette, if you have no money to put down, you must leave the game'.[1] This, however, is a little like the contention that we should never speak to others about Jesus Christ, but wait for the pure radiance of our virtuous lives to make itself felt. Unfortunately men might have to wait a very long time for this to happen, and perhaps there are services we can render in the meantime even while we remain sinners. If so we should not despise them, even while we despise ourselves. We are likely to go on for a lifetime being inadequate in Christian terms, and it would be depressing to reach the grave before getting started on being a little useful to others on that account.

What, then, are the positive aspects of this 'statement' activity, if any, and what are the preconditions for any utility it may possess? Perhaps it has become such an addiction that nothing you or I can say can alter its frequency or seriously impair its irrelevance. But we ought to try to clear our minds if only because, as we enter discussions and collaboration with our Roman Catholic friends, we must be able to explain what we are about.

It has an internal ecumenical value, as providing an oblique

[1] Colin Morris, *Include me out*, Epworth Press, 1968.

method for facing our own political divisions. But are we not now approaching the age of ecumenical maturity when we can endure a more candid confrontation? There are member churches in Arab lands, and others in lands favourable to the cause of Israel. Some churches are rooted in a political economy derived from Marxism, some in countries whose idol is pragmatism, some indebted to the Enlightenment. Is it necessary to continue the pretence that they can officially and formally agree on common policies for the hot issues of mankind? But if you surrender that pretence, do you not surrender with it the whole prospect of a serious ecumenical contribution to world community? The danger at least is that the ecumenical contribution will become a series of broad generalities interspersed with momentary and often misconceived passionate unanimities about a particular issue inadequately understood.

The clue here may be that throughout the churches we have tried to run before we have learned to walk. We have tried to translate too quickly our unity in Jesus Christ into terms of international political agreement. We have not yet reached the point ecclesiastically where we can together celebrate the eucharist. How can we imagine it possible that we can find a common understanding of the conflict in the Middle East? In our efforts to do so we run the risk of ending up with a formula which conceals our disunity while appearing to manifest our common mind.

This is an old and familiar problem to those experienced in ecumenical matters. They have sought a solution along several different lines. Everyone is agreed that pious generalities and vague exhortations to virtue have in the past too often exhausted the contribution of the churches. Most people are aware that the Gospel gives no sure guidance among the detailed technicalities of political decisions. But is there not a middle area where agreement might be reached—on something realistic and specific, on the general importance of economic development, the objective of disarmament, the necessity of creating supra-national political machinery and instruments to sustain a real international community, the right of self-determination?

Even here, however, it is difficult in practice to avoid the platitudinous. Few people in the world really wish to contest these worthy objectives openly and bluntly. When you come down to practical implementation the real arguments begin. We want economic development, but our balance of payments prevents us from being more generous. We want fair prices for raw materials but how can you stabilize them in a free market without doing more harm than good? We want disarmament, but if self-determination means anything it involves possessing the hardware to preserve one's national security. In practice we find that a list of agreed middle-ground objectives presents us with competing claims and contradictory policies. We are still several leagues away from the actual decisions that men have to make, so far away that we are not audible in an interesting respect when they come to make their minds up.

Another procedure has therefore been sought. What about getting together an ecumenical group of politically experienced Christians who had the knowledge and professional competence to go even further and to give advice even on the technicalities? This idea lay behind the creation of the Commission of the Churches on International Affairs, a body of men and women who had, not simply ideas and learning in the field of international politics, but in many cases actual experience of the decision-making process. This pattern has been repeated with modifications in the design of several national commissions of churches dealing with international affairs. The over-riding preoccupation was to find a way in which the churches could be very practical, and useful, actually contributing to the decision-making process, and not simply declaiming somewhat vainly at an unheeding world, applauded in the process only by the irrelevant faithful.

It ill behoves a servant of that Commission to attempt an evaluation of its work. All one can do is to indicate the questions the Commission itself is often forced to ask. First of all, how is it to take full advantage of its ecumenical fellowship, and enlarge its own mutual understanding, unless substantial resources of time and money are provided to allow it actually to meet regularly? Secondly, what authority has it?

The greater its technical and professional competence, the less it can speak in the name of all Christian people. If it goes into details of decision-making, it must be clear that it does not commit churches as a whole. If it avoids the details, its utility is vastly impaired. It must somehow retain the respect of the churches and their general confidence while at the same time leaving churches free to reserve their judgement about giving Christian authority to particular courses of action.

The choice whether to seek a world agreement on the price of copper, and thus attempt to stabilize the economy of Zambia, is one which churches cannot feel confident in making. Will it have the desired effect? Will everybody begin switching to the use of aluminium? Can all the main suppliers be induced to co-operate? All these are the elements which go into the making of truly responsible decisions. The simple, generous desire to assist Zambia is only the beginning of the matter. But that desire remains a fruitless sentimentality until someone translates it into serious technical proposals. And these proposals will depend for their efficacy more on skilled judgement, shrewd forecasting, a wise understanding of 'how things actually work out' than on specifically Christian virtues.

Christians can help to create the atmosphere of seriousness, drive and determination in which technical solutions are sought. They cannot, in the name of the churches, agree to underwrite the validity of the technical solutions which emerge. But at the same time they can scarcely stand back and excuse themselves just at the point where real decisions have to be taken. So here is the dilemma. Is an ecumenical instrument confined to setting the stage for other men to reach decisions on? Or can it share the burden of ambiguous decisions without according them a Christian authority they do not merit?

The churches have, up to now, accorded their Commission on International Affairs a considerable measure of independence just to meet this point. In a sense it is a device for preserving equally the independence of the churches from too close an entanglement with political detail. The Commission must win the general confidence of churches, but must not pretend to commit them in support of all its detailed operations. It is a very delicate relationship, which can be sustained only so long as it is lubricated by a large measure of personal trust and understanding. But, if it works, it represents a new experiment in ecclesiastical institutional life. For in effect what happens is this. The churches create an instrument from their own resources, to serve the world in a particularly sensitive area, and they set it relatively free of their own institutions so that it can do its job of service better. In so doing they manifest a unique Christian selflessness, and impose a great burden of responsibility. Both are qualities we ought to know something special about.

So far we have been exploring ways to deal with the fact that ecumenical unity does not simply translate into political unity. We know all too well how agonizing it is in critical situations to have to acknowledge this fact. Those who have struggled with the conflicts between India and Pakistan, India and its hill tribes of Nagaland, Nigeria and Biafra, Indonesia and Malaysia besides the great over-arching opposition of East and West, realize that the idea of bringing together, at the height of crisis, Christians from each side is a naïve proposal. They are either too much identified with their cause to accept a radical confrontation, or so prepared to see the other side as to be regarded as traitors to their own. At that point it is either too late or too early to submit the fragile bonds of ecumenism to full political strain. One needs a wiser opportunism which quickly exploits a season of advantage and makes the most of it, either to forestall or to repair hostilities.

This brings us to another device which has worked better in the hands of national ecumenical groupings like the British Council of Churches than it has so far in a wider context. I refer to the study in depth by a specialist working party of a particular international problem. Dr. Ian Ramsey, the Bishop of Durham, has paid tribute to the work of the B.C.C. International Department in this respect, under the encouraging title 'Making a Tradition'. The Evangelical Church in Germany has pioneered even more courageously in sponsoring its own group to report on the problem of Germany's eastern frontiers. This 'Denkschrift' not only exposed its authors to commendation and villification on a heroic scale: it exposed them thus precisely because such candour and honesty on so bitterly controversial a subject was liable to have real political consequences. In the event, it had this effect, and is widely credited for having opened up the first possibility to 'mention the unmentionable' in the search for reconciliation in central Europe.

The 'Conference on Church and Society' sponsored by the World Council of Churches produced a unique variant of this. Many people have noted that the section of the report of that conference, dealing with world economic development, was of outstanding quality. Obviously in the somewhat chaotic conditions of a huge conference no such thing as a 'working party' could hope to do original study. But there were present economists and specialists from various countries who had long been engaged in the problems of development. They found it relatively easy to put together from their own previous researches a body of agreed material which the rest of the conference, conscious of its relative inexpertness, happily accepted. This was a case of ecumenical crystallization rather than of original creation. It represented the fact that scholarly thinking, secular as well as religious, had reached a broad measure of agreement in this field. What the churches could do was to advertise the fact.

Why have we not done more ecumenically in this field? The first and simple answer must be that it is expensive, both in time and money. Bringing a working party together nationally demands the time of busy experts, but they can work over a meal or in the evening without major disruptions. It is totally different internationally. The operation must be of such assured consequence that men and women will give days at a time, to travel, and then to protracted but business-like discussion. Leadership must be first class to identify the right questions, control a wide-ranging debate, and crystallize discoveries. Nevertheless, while the requirements are formidable it may well be asked whether any alternative method offers equal prospects of making a worthy contribution to international decisions. At least it offers escape from the recurrent experience of finding ourselves trying to resolve the insoluble because we came too late on the scene and have not done our homework.

But when we produce our statements, create our Commissions, produce the reports of our working parties, who listens or reads? Or, more precisely, how does our activity relate to the actual procedure of decision-making? This raises a more profound question— what is the proper function of the churches in relation to those exercising political power in the world?

That is the subject of the next chapter.

3 Are Governments Evil?

It is always possible to consign governments to the class of hopeless cases on whom it is impossible to exercise any effective reforming influence. Churches have done this for all sorts of reasons. The most attractive, to themselves, is a sort of theological argument. Governments represent power, and power, in the eyes of Christian realists, is a very corrupting thing. It is the source of pride and arrogance, and leads men away from the sensitivities of a truly humane relation to their fellows. Men with power are so busy manipulating others that they soon come to regard them as pawns.

Then again we can enjoy the luxury of repenting of our forefathers' sins in this respect, a repentance which need not be too costly to our own self-esteem. The churches seem to have been so identified with the political establishment in past ages that they have betrayed their own non-conforming duty in the world. So runs the argument—and now, with the fortunate arrival on the scene of a new Christian generation like ourselves, there is the prospect that a genuine, radical independency can be established. For anyone who knows church history, and particularly for those who have studied with respect the long tradition of Christian radical sects, this is certainly an over-simplified picture.

The historical lessons to be drawn are correspondingly misunderstood. For there had been in fact a continual oscillation between a conception of Christianity so radical and utopian as to lose all practical connexion with statecraft, and a type of Christian accommodation to the powers that be which simply supplies a religious blessing to the *status quo*. In between the two extremes all sorts of permutations of the relation of church and government, faith and politics have been explored. The question is not a new one, although much contemporary argument seems based on the assumption that no one has seriously or honestly thought about it before. But we must, as true non-conformists, seek the original and novel answer that fits our particular times and circumstances.

It is not really very original or novel to take the position of being detached, cynical and negative about governments. Indeed quite the contrary—this is the fashion of our egalitarian and mildly anarchic times. For the sort of optimistic liberalism which has been the underlying philosophy of the post-war world found it difficult to appreciate that society is and will remain full of real contradictions and conflicts which cannot be simply resolved. People therefore did not recognize that the authority of government is required to avoid complete social stalemate leading on to the violence of frustration. It is one of the hopeful signs of the revolt of the younger generation that part of it is restoring some realism again to our political thinking, after the bland sentimentalities of a superficial secular humanism.

This revolt is asking the right questions when it recognizes that power is both inevitable and necessary in a society, and goes on to investigate how it can be made responsive to the real needs of men. This is to take government seriously again. Those on the other hand who try to perpetuate the old dream of the withering away of the state, or attempt to give it new interpretation in the form of perpetual revolution, are setting off down a blind alley which Christian sects have often previously explored to their discomfiture.

What does it mean, then, that Christians should be non-conformist in relation to governments? Or rather, to keep within the narrower purpose of this book, what should be the attitude of official church bodies to governments? Perhaps it is useful to start with an illustration.

Robert Kennedy left in note form an account of the Cuba crisis of October 1962, as seen from within the White House. Allowance must be made for an element of fraternal piety in Robert Kennedy's portrait of his brother. An active and competitive political personality, such as the Senator was at the time, must always have an eye to the political effect of what he writes. But I have talked with one or two of the key personalities involved and have found a very impressive confirmation that in broad terms this was how things happened, and how men behaved in one of the most critical governmental actions of our century.

He records from memory how the President reflected agonizingly to him his own sense of the awful choices ahead:

'He talked about the miscalculations that lead to war. War is rarely intentional. The Russians don't wish to fight any more than we do. They do not want to war with us nor we with them. And yet if events continue as they have in the last several days that struggle—which no one wishes, which will accomplish nothing—will engulf and destroy all mankind.

'He wanted to make sure he had done everything in his power, everything conceivable, to prevent such a catastrophe. Every opportunity was to be given to the Russians to find a peaceful settlement which would not diminish their national security or be a public humiliation. It was not only for Americans that he was concerned, or primarily for the older generation . . . but for the children whose lives would be snuffed out like everyone else's.'

The inner group of advisers was divided as to whether or not the missile sites on Cuba should be quickly destroyed.

'Again and again he (the President) emphasized that we must understand the implications of every step. What response could we anticipate? What were the implications for us? . . . These hourly decisions, necessarily made with such rapidity, could be made only by the President of the United States, but any one of them might close and lock doors for peoples and governments in many other lands. We had to be aware that the President was deciding for the United States, the Soviet Union, Turkey, Nato, and really for all mankind. . . . Those hours in the Cabinet Room that Saturday afternoon in October could never be erased from the minds of any of us. . . . We won't attack tomorrow, the President said, we will try again.'

Not all government decisions have to be taken in such apocalyptic circumstances, nor are they taken on such an exalted plane. But the extreme case vividly illumines the processes of government, and helps us to see them as something which men do, men of flesh and blood like ourselves. What part should the churches play at such a time, in relation to government? These men in the Cabinet Room, on a Saturday afternoon, may have had on the table a message from the churches which ran:

'Taking their stand on statements made by the World Council Assemblies, Committees and Officers of the World Council of Churches have on several occasions expressed their concern and regret when governments have taken unilateral military action against other governments. The Officers of the World Council of Churches consider it therefore their duty to express their grave concern and regret concerning the action which the USA Government has felt it necessary to take with regard to Cuba and fervently hope that every government concerned will exercise the greatest possible restraint in order to avoid a worsening of the situation.'

It must be admitted that the message was probably never read by those in the Cabinet Room. It may never have got so far. But if it did, would it have added anything of consequence to the argument going on there? Looking back from a distance, one is not passionately convinced that, at a moment of truly universal crisis, perhaps the turning point towards sanity in the nuclear confrontation of the super powers, the message was worthy of the occasion, or on a level equivalent to the sombre but deeply responsible debate going on round that historic table. One almost acknowledges that its effect was to trivialize a profound human experience, to accommodate within some casuistry regarding unilateral action what was rather a supreme effort to stabilize the relation of the super powers.

Be that as it may—and as Christians we ought to know something about penitence—there is a more precise lesson to be learnt. There was nothing original or non-conformist in an attitude of the churches which was suspicious of America. That is always the fate of the very powerful and one which is perfectly understandable. We know each other well enough, and some of us know ourselves sufficiently, to view with anxiety anyone gaining real control over others. We know we cannot be trusted, in that situation, normally to attend to the interests of those we control with anything like the enthusiasm we devote to our own. There is nothing particularly Christian in that discovery. Most hard-headed people reach the same conclusion on the basis of observation. Christian originality consists simply in the realization that the rule applies to ourselves as well as to other people. In the case of the Cuba crisis it was no doubt mainly the universality of the impending disaster that enabled a government with overwhelming power to attempt to use it for the general good.

The non-conformist, the original, the surprising thing would have been if the churches had escaped from the general human mood of that time, and had found their own particular rôle. Men swing in their moods from an excessive and debasing respect for political power to an equally exaggerated contempt of it. Christian non-conformity involves avoiding both, and doing the hard thing. It requires us to recognize the reality and responsibility of power without being in the least taken in by its pretensions. The impression the Cuba event leaves, after the lapse of years, is that the churches failed in that proper non-conformity. They were too much impressed with the pretentions of great power to take its responsibilities seriously. They had not enough independence of their day and age to see beyond the universal human anxiety to the underlying realities. So their action sounds now a little querulous, at a time when anything 'little' was singularly out of place.

Why does such a thing occur? Amongst many possible answers, I mention one which is normally unmentionable. Human institutions are like the male of the species. When they are healthy there is in their make up an inbuilt rivalry and competitiveness towards other institutions performing in the same field. Church bodies are often far too small and, in the public secular domain, too insignificant to rival governments, or to feel that in any sense they have a comparable responsibility for public affairs. But when they become ecumenical they begin to see things differently. They develop ideas about what is the right policy in regard to South Africa, nuclear arms, the United Nations. They want these policies to prevail. It is the obstinacy and unreceptiveness of governments which prevents this happening. So a rivalry is set up which leads to an attitude of mutual suspicion with a certain amount of resentment thrown in. That is the moment to ask searching questions about whether we have got a fresh and lively notion of what the relation ought to be, or whether we are stupidly blundering forward with a set of assumptions conforming to some outdated situations of the past.

I believe myself that one of the misleading factors has been the result of trying to fit ourselves into the pattern of operations developed at the newly emerging United Nations. What is the proper rôle of the churches, or their corporate ecumenical agency, at the UN? For many years the formal answer has been that the churches agency was a 'non-governmental organization related to the Economic and Social Council in Category B'. Now whatever that means, it has certainly no visible connection with any definition of the church known to the New Testament—'A people for God's own possession', 'A royal priesthood', 'A holy nation'. Instead, the simple practical thing has been to conform to a pattern set by others, and content ourselves with being regarded as a voluntary society, akin in some respects to a political pressure group, pre-occupied with religious affairs but believing they have political implications. Non-governmental organizations exist as a rule to exercise such influence as they can on governmental organizations.

So the scene is set for the rivalry I have portrayed. But to escape, it is going to be necessary to spell out a very original and peculiar rôle for the churches. They do not conform to any known category, in relation to governments, though they are continually falling into the temptation to do so. Sometimes they seem to become part of the government itself—'the Conservative Party at prayer'. Sometimes they identify themselves with the more utopian of the radicals—'the Tribune wearing a halo'. There are always theologians available to prove that one or other position is a necessary consequence of Christian faith. They explain why the church should in this particular situation conform to the enthusiastic expectations of its ardent political wooers.

And yet it is precisely here that fundamental Christian non-conformity is needed. The whole of mankind is the concern of the churches—governing and governed, rich and poor, sinner and saint (if you insist on the parallel). But that does not mean that ecclesiastical leaders are better able to do other people's jobs than they are themselves. Indeed the contrary is true in history. We are vividly aware of the danger of a government taking upon itself to order the affairs of the churches. We ought to be equally aware of the fatal results when church leaders start trying to control political decisions. It is very hard to think of a single instance when the result has not been both incompetent and potentially tyrannous.

What then are we left with? True Christian non conformity in the relation of churches and governments—ecumenical bodies and the great inter-governmental organs of our day—is much more complex than we realize. That is why we are for ever over-simplifying it in the heat and excitement of the moment. Churches are neither anti-government, nor pro-government in principle, nor are they properly to regard themselves as a sort of shadow government, although they must at times appear to be a bit of all three. We shall

27

look at each in turn. But the concept we ought to explore, which is peculiarly our own, peculiarly original and uniquely non-conformist, is the concept of a chaplaincy in all three guises. A chaplaincy implies at once an element of real identification and at the same time a certain detachment and distance. It is a rôle that is fundamentally humble, the rôle of a servant, and at the same time the rôle of independent witness, ready to speak disturbingly. Let us be more specific.

In its responsibility to those who govern, the church needs a maturity which frees it from self-conscious awe in dealing with those who are powerful in the world. The spiritual freedom of those who know that their ultimate loyalty lies beyond all the panoply of earthly power, should give us a capacity to consort with and understand those who possess that power. We can well appreciate that human wills are so strong, so diverse, so readily in conflict that a society needs a final arbiter if corporate decisions are ever to be taken and effectively implemented. That means some are having power to act for—and over—all in practical affairs, if a society is to move and develop.

No doubt people who rise to positions of power tend to be those who enjoy that sort of life. So they are particularly prone to dominate, to believe in their own judgement as better than others, to develop a protective insensibility to the human cost to others of what they set in motion or neglect. In any case, not being omnipotent, they pay regard to all the other groups and interests who have the capacity to make life difficult for them. So they are often more alert to the demands of other power groups than to the cries of the helpless. They have to be, in order to do their jobs effectively. That is their occupational hazard. It goes with the position and there is no way of avoiding the risk, though there are prophylactics.

The church is, or should be, one such. Yet it cannot act effectively as chaplain and prophylactic, if it feels entirely exterior to the whole operation of government. It is only from a truly imaginative sharing of the experience of governmental responsibility that we can find the way to do any peculiar task relevantly or effectively. So there is both involvement and detachment. The illustration of the Cuba crisis suggests an action by the churches which lacked a true greatness at that moment because it seemed so remote from the real experience of men round a White House table one October Saturday afternoon.

Does this mean that the churches should so share governmental responsibility that, in effect, they constitute themselves a sort of shadow government? This appears to be suggested by deliverances from churches on precise issues of policy—whether or not Britain should reopen negotiations with the Smith régime in Rhodesia, whether her defence policy should include the retention, the sharing, or the abandonment of a nuclear armoury, what initiatives she should take in the Middle East. I have elsewhere given my opinion on this matter in the general formula—'the task of the churches is to deepen the debate on such issues, not to attempt itself to conclude it'. But this is not at all easy in practice. Only by making some clear distinctions can we avoid pushing the churches back into the sort of pious platitudes which have so often spoiled their interventions in the past.

First, to be a 'chaplain' to governments means making a serious effort to share at a professional level their actual dilemmas. We must understand—or we must sustain a specialist group from amongst us which attempts to understand—what the real choices are. Such a group does not have the final responsibility for decision making, and must guard itself from the pretentiousness of suggesting otherwise. But it ought to know enough to ask the right questions, to urge attention to human considerations easily overlooked, and even if possible to come up with original proposals. We shall see later what it means to say that truth and humanity are to be its guiding lights. This is a pastoral task, not that of a pressure group. For that reason we must be particularly suspicious of any ecclesiastical tendency to give the weight of church authority to a particular line of action. There is no such thing as a 'Christian' policy in that sense, and to imply that there is merely injects a fanaticism and intolerance into the public debate which is the first step towards religious wars.

It is quite another thing that Christians as citizens should band themselves together with others like-minded, to fight relentlessly for a policy they believe in. This is a sign of true commitment to political life. It involves devotion to a cause, however relative, and the risking of a choice, however uncertain, as the only conceivable way of doing our public duty. We join parties, or create new ones. Within such groups we struggle for particular actions which we believe will maximize economic justice, racial harmony, the prospects of avoiding war, or whatever. We may be proved wrong in our prescriptions. We may have to adopt means which are ambiguous. But those who wait for perfect conditions never get started. The one thing we must not do is suggest or imply that what we support is in some simple way the will of God, the only possible course for a Christian, the policy of the churches. That is to claim a certainty for our fallible judgements they do not deserve, and a perception of God's will which is not available to men. And it is to act in the name of a lot of men and women we have not consulted.

The real danger is that professional ecumenical 'chaplaincy' groups confuse their rôle with that of the political activists, and in a moment of aberration try to commit 'the church' to what they themselves recommend. On such occasions it is perfectly in order for a government to ask them 'Who are you—whom do you really represent?' And it is necessary to confess that many of the 'positions' taken up by such groups, which claim the authority of large ecumenical communities, reflect the tactical skill of their sponsors rather than the deep felt conviction of the Christian community as a whole.

So much for the element of pro-government or shadow government in the rôle of the churches. What of the anti-government? This is perhaps the easiest and happiest and most natural activity for the nonconforming Christian. For every crumb of Christian compassion we are granted, and every exciting glimpse we have of the unbounded generosity of God, moves us to cry out with the poor and needy, and those who have no helper, for the attention of the powers that be. So engrossed do the latter appear to be with visions of irrelevant grandeur, so abstract in their calculations from the flesh and blood realities of ordinary human life, so cynical in their acceptance of the *status quo*, so content with the levers of power in their hands, that anyone who calls himself a 'chaplain' of humanity must long to join some visible manifestation of protest. Here surely is a rôle the churches must not neglect if they are to remain loyal to the gospel.

The only caveat is connected with our capacity to corrupt even the highest of our spiritual gifts. It is, for instance, very easy at the present time to seek not so much justice for men as prestige and contemporaneity for the church by allying her with popular sentiment. What is more simple in a day when men find the church as an institution marvellously irrelevant and readily disposable than to plan a 'come-back' by setting ourselves at the head of a mass protest movement, which incidentally, we have not started? It has been done, in my view, in recent years, although we have not acknowledged even to ourselves exactly what we are up to. How ultimately horrifying it would be if we used the cries of suffering men as a vehicle for our own institutional advancement!

The other aspect of the matter is that once we are seriously burdened with the plight of men, the danger of war, the prevalence of misery and starvation, protest will never be enough. We must also press on to the point where we can see how the levers of real power, governmental power, could be operated to provide relief. And so we are back at the starting point again, with the need to deal with the wielders of power in terms relevant to their situation, but perhaps with a new dynamism and restlessness disturbing our governmental chaplaincy.

The church, the Christian community, the ecumenical fellowship should in principle seethe with the never-ending struggle between those called to shout from the housetops of the crying needs of the world, and those who find their vocation in association with the men of power. It should be a community in which this confrontation is creative and patient, even if passionate, where we recognize each other in Christ, really listen to each other for a change instead of preaching at each other, and out of the strife and struggle perform better our chaplaincy to the world in all its diverse parts.

All of this simply illustrates our confusion in answering the question put by a government official to whom representation is made—'Who are you?' Who, indeed? A self appointed 'cabinet' of amateur politicians, taking itself more seriously than is justified? The official representatives of the churches, authorized to speak in the name of the Christian constituency? A prophetic cell speaking for God?

Evidently what we need is a theological definition of the church and of the 'secular' powers, and a thought out, defensible, theological understanding of the proper relation of the one to the other. We used to have such a defensible position—or at least a set of respectable alternatives—which guided thoughtful men in the relatively cosy and traditional world of Europe. History had forced men to think about it since the time of Constantine, through the period of Empire and Papacy, right up to the establishments (and disestablishments) of the modern period. It cannot be said that the Anglo-Saxon mind has lately revealed any great acuteness or profundity in dealing with the issue. Indeed the muddle and emotionalism surrounding the discussion is nicely reflected in the confused way the churches approach governments in actual practice. But we shall not get much farther till we discipline ourselves to think the matter through theologically. And in view of the dominance of English speaking churches in the ecumenical programme in this field, the World Council of Churches itself will tend to stagger around uncertainly till we have thought out what we are doing, and who we are.

What was useful in the Western Church in Europe is now no longer enough. Ecumenically we are powerfully influenced by two quite other traditions. There is on the one hand the tradition of Eastern Orthodoxy, where the church has always had a sort of intimate relation with the secular power. And on the other, there is the American solution where that relation has been consciously rejected in favour of a separation of church and state. Moreover, a worldwide Christian community is, in large areas of Asia and elsewhere, neither large enough nor deeply enough rooted in society to pretend to any serious partnership with the state. So precedents set by the peculiar history of mediaeval Europe no longer suffice. The temptation is to adopt positions based not so much on biblical and theological insight as on tactical convenience. This is the temptation which needs to be powerfully and freshly resisted.

This book affords no occasion to do much more than point to the task. But to set it going it may help to quote some words of Bonhoeffer which indicate the depth of what we are talking about:

'Thy Kingdom come! That is the prayer which the pious soul of the person who flees from the world cannot say; nor can the Utopian, the fanatic, the impassioned reformer. It can only be the prayer of the children of the world, who do not set themselves apart, who have no miraculous recipes for making everything better, who are not superior to the world, but in its midst in this daily round, are deeply subject to it, persevering together because it is precisely by doing so that they are faithful to life and fixing their gaze on that one place in the world where they are struck with wonder to see the lifting of the curse, the profound assent given by God to the world's plea: that one place where, in the midst of this dying, broken, thirsting world, the resurrection

of Christ can be seen by whoever can believe in it.... The Kingdom
of God is the *Kingdom of the Resurrection* on earth.'[1]

Bonhoeffer never thinks of the Kingdom (as we so often do)
as other than the coming of God himself:

'How will the Kingdom of God come to us? No differently from
God himself; in the destruction of the law of death, in the
resurrection, in miracle, and yet, at the same time, in the affirma-
tion of the world, in an entry into its own order, its communities,
its history. The two are interlinked. For it is only where the
world is wholly accepted that it can be truly broken and destroyed;
and only the lifting of the curse on the earth makes it possible to
take that earth really seriously.'

It is only in this context that he will consider the relation of
church and state:

'Miracle and order—these are the two forms under which the
Kingdom of God appears on earth, the two forms of its twofold
and distinct manifestation. Miracle, as a breaking of all our
orders, and order as the support of what is ordered to the miraculous. But miracle is also surrounded by the world of order,
and order keeps itself complete, in its limitations, through miracle.
The form in which the Kingdom of God appears as miracle we
call the Church; the form in which it appears as order we call the
State.'

To many contemporary minds the idea comes as a novelty
that the state is, or ever could be, an aspect of the Kingdom of
God. Yet it is in such a way that theology can render service by
calling into question some of the accepted assumptions of an age.
It requires Christian nerve, and a readiness to sacrifice popularity,
thus to challenge the easy utopianisms of our time, and it is this
'nerve' which is presently lacking. Yet without a radical theological
integrity of this nature we shall never approach a Christian understanding of the way church and state properly limit each other's
action.

Bonhoeffer on a later page of the same book puts it thus:

[1] Gessammelte Schriften III, pp. 273–8, quoted in *Bonhoeffer—the man and
his work*, by René Marle, S.J. translated by Rosemary Sheed, Geoffrey
Chapman, 1968.

'In proclaiming the commandment and the grace of God, the Church stands at the limit of human possibilities, which has been penetrated from above. But, in that it speaks of the penetration of the limit, of the laws of the world, while standing itself as a human institution completely within this limit, it points to these laws, these orders of the world, to whose annihilation, destruction and ending through God, it so powerfully testifies. The preaching of the Church is therefore necessarily "political", i.e. it is directed at the order of politics in which man is engaged. But precisely because it is "political" it is primarily concerned with the critical limit of all political action. The Church is the limit of politics and therefore eminently political and a-political at the same time. Because the Church testifies to the penetration of the limit, it points to the limit, to the law, to order, to the State. The Church limits the State, the State limits the Church.'

Such a position is far removed from the fashionable notions of today which seek greater freedom for the church by drawing a sharp line of separation between church and state. This used to be an aim of Christian nonconformity in Britain. The contemporary form of nonconformity is surely in the other direction—to seek the proper relation rather than to press for separation. One reason is that we have seen in practice how unreal separation really is. Many would assent to the judgement of Bonhoeffer writing from America in 1939 and giving his assessment of the American experiment of separation thus:

' . . . the separation of Church and State does not result in the Church continuing to apply itself to its own task; it is no guarantee against secularisation. Nowhere is the Church more secularised than where it is separated in principle, as it is here. This very separation can create an opposition, so that the Church engages much more strongly in political and secular things.'

The opposition is one we have already noticed as already an element in our thinking as we have allowed ourselves to be conformed, unwittingly, to the false assumptions of our time.

4 The Power of the Church

The taunt to which we are peculiarly sensitive in church circles is that of 'ineffectiveness'. We cannot easily endure the overtones and undertones of that description. It conjures up images of vapid, windy sermonizers, creating fantasy worlds of complacent self-esteem wholly unrelated to the manly business of living in this world. We know well enough that this description has often been merited in church life in the past, and we secretly fear that it may be truer today than we realize. So we go to great lengths to show that it need not be the case. We want to be effective in a way that matters in secular terms. We want newspapers and television to pay attention to us, to report what we say and do, particularly in respect of public affairs. We hate the thought of being irrelevant, and, even worse, the thought that other people can easily dismiss us as irrelevant. We want to be a fighting, witnessing, news-creating church, and we will go to some lengths to satisfy ourselves that this is in fact what we are.

We want to be where the action is. This is surely a right instinct. For where men are making choices of action, they are declaring their ultimate allegiances and, whether they know it or not, they are denying or recognizing the Lordship of Jesus Christ. 'Not every one that *says* Lord, Lord . . . but he that doeth the will of my Father' (Matthew 7: 21). Where men are doing things, committing themselves and their futures to truly serious courses of action, there is one place at any rate where the church should be.

Revolutionary movements in Latin America and the response of the establishment to them—that is such a place. The long, uneven African recruitment to challenge white supremacy in the southern continent, and the arrogant, anxious, or resolute white response—

that is another such place. Where men struggle for their moral and intellectual integrity in a régime which attempts to control the thoughts of men's minds—there is another. For in every such case men are facing choices and committing themselves to historical decisions which contain implicit answers to the question: 'Who do you say that I am?' (Matthew 15: 16).

I have not attempted to exhaust the list of contemporary crisis points. Great issues of peace and war may be involved in decisions facing Great Britain regarding her place in Europe. What the wealthy nations do about speeding up economic development elsewhere and reorganizing fundamentally the patterns of world trade will be decisive for the human race. So one could go on adding to the list. For the moment, however, I want to use some of these issues simply to pose the questions—what power has the church, what power ought the church to have, what 'effectiveness' can the church display at such critical moments?

To be there, where the action is—that is the minimal requirement for a serious involvement in the world. Yet is it still a revolutionary idea for our churches. Kind and contented, the haven of comfort for the suburban household, worthy in producing qualities of generosity, stability, humanity within their own privileged society, so many of our churches are light years removed from the blood and dust and agonies of the human struggle. It is hard to imagine their respectable precincts being invaded by the passionate, terrible conflicts of the 'outside' world. Yet it is precisely this invasion which some of the younger generation insistently and properly demand—an end to the cosiness, and an exposure to the reality of conflict, the sort of conflict which can draw blood.

The protest of youth has no doubt a thousand different voices in it—the cry of a generation raised in affluence but facing a world full of doom, the impatience of those unaccustomed to having the satisfaction of their wants postponed facing the obduracies of human society, the self-righteousness of those who perceive the sense of guilt of their elders. But one voice we dare not miss. It is the demand of youth for realism and for humanity. It involves a fierce criticism of a society obsessed by its own ingenuity in technical developments and blind to the depersonalized, dehumanized and cruel consequences of its cleverness. Above all, it is a criticism of a society which has lost the capacity to be fundamentally critical of itself.

Out of this emerges the demand that the church be not found

wanting and ineffective at a cross-roads of history. It must be where the action is, not in a dusty Victorian pew. It must itself be revolutionary, and must ally itself unashamedly with the revolutionary movements of our day. The power of the church, for too long used to sustain the *status quo*, must now be switched to the radicals, and be seen to be committed to their cause. A whole 'theology of revolution' is already being worked at, to give ideological foundations to the new party line. Incidentally one is constantly amazed at the compliance of well-intentioned theologians, who, once a new political fashion has emerged, are ready to decorate it with the necessary theological spangles. It is remarkable that they so rarely manage to point out these new theological insights ahead of time, before the secular world has arrived at them from totally different presuppositions.

We are thus confronted with two different assertions which are constantly entangled with each other. One is crucial to any future of the Christian faith. The other, slipping in surreptitiously under the same umbrella, is of much more doubtful quality. The first assertion takes seriously that Jesus Christ entered into the very middle of human history, where the action was. His birth got mixed up with a statistical survey by an imperial government. His life was lived amongst people running their own anti-imperial underground movement. His death was the result of factional in-fighting in his own revolutionary people, and the political 'wisdom' of the occupying power. The one thing about it all that is certainly untrue is that the events had any remote, detached 'religiousness' about them such as belongs to so much of our church life.

If ever there was a religion which conformed to no other generally accepted notion of religion it is Christianity. Far from providing an escape, a recompense, or a salve in face of the agonies of human history it rather offers the resources to take them at last with open-eyed commitment. The young are right who say that if the church is ineffective at the critical places in our modern world, no amount of 'going to church' will save us from our proper liquidation.

But then there is slipped in a more doubtful proposition—that in the struggles of our day the only way for the church to be effective is to take sides. To be where the action is—that can still be no more than adopting the rôle of a spectator or commentator. What is needed is the energy of participants, those prepared to do the fighting with the hosts of light against the powers of darkness.

37

That is what many people are looking for from the church at this point in history, and they make it clear that their remaining respect for the church depends on whether or not it is prepared to commit itself thus.

Papal encyclicals such as 'Pacem in terris' or 'Populorum progressio' are carefully analysed to see if a new political commitment is implied, or only the discarding of a reactionary old one. The 'Church and Society' conference under the auspicies of the World Council of Churches is assessed—by serious people who have no necessary Christian allegiance—to discover if a new weight is being thrown into the political balance of mankind. And all of this generalized attention stems from the fact of the ecumenical movement itself. The mere possibility of joint Christian action is potentially of real political significance. Simply that such a bloc of the human race might be brought to a common political mind is important to anyone calculating the power structures of the world. The prospect begins to beckon that the church itself might be a political force to be reckoned with.

Is this a prospect that the church, through its accredited central organs, should pursue? It would be no great historical novelty if it did. We all know what the power of the mediaeval papacy could accomplish when the political structures of Europe's dark ages were in confusion and disarray. Are we now, on an international and universal scale, entering a new period of chaos and disruption when the political structures are quite inadequate for human needs, but not yet open to the kind of rebuilding supranationally that the times require?

This is a haunting question when the ecumenical reality offers new ecclesiastical possibilities, as yet dimly apprehended. Is it the task of the whole church in the whole world to grasp some of the levers of power so ineffectually or competitively operated by a dying outmoded political system? Should the church be seen to be committed to certain political objectives, and should it pursue them realistically but in its own discreet and peculiar way? Certainly the idea appeals at various levels. For one thing it would ensure that the church was noticed—that it was recognized as relevant. It would fit in nicely with a world which sees in politics the road to human salvation. It would seem a logical and necessary consequence of all that has been said about the Lordship of Christ over the whole of human life, the taking seriously of the secular world.

But look for a moment at some of the possibilities. A special correspondent writing in the *Christian Herald* in November 1968 had this to say of the situation in Tanzania: 'Communist China has for years been trying to spread its influence in many of the Black African nations, and nowhere is it trying harder than in Tanzania, the one-party state of President Julius Nyerere. But in that country one of the major stumbling blocks to its aims of more ideological and economic influence is the Catholic Church, which is a power in the land and which has considerable support from the President.'

The correspondent describes the influx of Chinese instructors and economic aid into the country but adds that 'a far more concrete example of the Red threat can be seen in the existence of guerrilla training camps, with a steady output of terrorists who arrive from all parts of Black Africa for training'. Over against this he sets the fact that 'the Church is well-established and is playing an important rôle in Tanzania's development. More than two million of the country's twelve million population are Catholics and the Church runs more than 1400 schools and 25 hospitals . . . '.

The article is open to objection on many grounds. For one thing it is highly doubtful whether President Nyerere sees matters in that light at all. For another the assumption of Catholic versus Communist seems to derive from a period before Pope John and his encyclical 'Pacem in Terris' wherein he sought a different type of relation to the Communist world than is here implied. But for our purposes the question to be raised is another one altogether. Is our objection that the politics of the writer are reactionary and obscurantist? Would it be all right to cast the church in this rôle of an effective political power in a given situation, so long as it took the 'right' side? Another article could then be written to show how the church's resources, of schools, hospitals, faithful membership, and influence were being used in the service of African liberation movements, welcoming such help as the Chinese or other people were prepared to offer in a common cause. Would that make it all right, if it were true?

This is by no means an academic question. Indeed it is one of the questions that lies unanswered behind heated debates in our churches and missionary societies, our British Council of Churches and the organs of the World Council of Churches. And since the struggle for justice in southern Africa is going to preoccupy men's minds for many years to come, it is going to be a main question at issue for the foreseeable future. To what extent can the church commit itself and its membership to political ends and means? And can it properly seek to exercise power in the political arena? Should it lend support to the concept of a united Europe, as a step towards supra-nationalism? Or alternatively, should it campaign for self-determination, in a region such as Biafra? Should it seek to ensure that India does not become a nuclear power? Or should it commit itself to a policy of securing a fixed and fair price for the primary commodities of the developing world, free from the pressures of the market place?

All of these policies have their Christian champions, and a zealous champion sees advantage in getting some kind of ecclesiastical endorsement for his views.

Instinctively we have an aversion to the idea of the political church. We have been well taught that in the records we possess of the ministry of Jesus, He is represented as deliberately abjuring a political career. It is possible to argue that His was a unique messianic vocation, not to be compared exactly to ours. All the evidence is that His strong temptation to present himself as a political saviour was curiously similar to ours—the desire to be relevant, the advantage of conforming to general expectations, the possibility of bringing real bread to hungry people and justice to the oppressed. He recruited political zealots to His team, but He had to disappoint them at the crucial moment. One can understand Peter's despair at the politically disastrous step of letting the authorities crucify the leader in circumstances when the crowds would certainly not be on His side. There was no sense in it.

Moreover we have seen in history how, when the church exercises political power, the result is a terrible threat to men. Of course we can always assure ourselves that things will be different this time. It is characteristic of the revolutionary and messianic age we live in to assume that this generation is free from the faults that afflicted those who went before. But it is, to say the least, an unlikely assumption. And objectively there are reasons why a political church, exercising power, is always a human threat. It tends inevitably to cover with a cloak of moral absolutism what are essentially ambiguous and conditional judgements. By giving a religious dimension to a political choice, the church obscures the fact that men of integrity and intelligence may reach a different conclusion perfectly properly. The effect of this is to prejudice serious political debate, to bless the closed mind, and to promote fanaticism. Yet in our changing, dynamic world nothing is politically more important than open-ness to what is new, humility before an alternative opinion, and the recognition that all our political devices are provisional and subject to revision.

Put in another way, the commitment which is absolute for the church is a commitment to faith in a person. All other commitments are provisional and subject to this over-riding one. A man is often required to commit his actions irrecoverably to a particular opinion, to throw himself after what he believes to be the best course of action. But the Christian who does this can never console himself that he is infallibly right to do so. His act of self-commitment is also a throwing of himself on the judgement and the forgiveness of his Lord. For nothing that he can do in the political field—full of factual uncertainty, ambiguous consequence and very limited possibility—is on the same level as the perfection of Jesus Christ.

One of the great dangers of our new-found interest in the secular world is that the church will bring into the political field a degree of intolerance, an absolutism, and a moral pharisaism which renders all reasonable dialogue fruitless, and which is an enemy of the compromise which politics is all about. For the art of politics is to find ways in which differing wills and interests can co-operate in reasonable degree and avoid head-on collisions. But the temptation of the church is to try to decide what is right, and then make everyone else agree. This is not politics. It is tyranny.

Then again, when we don the robe of the political church, we like to imagine ourselves as free from the gross self-interest of nations and governments, determined only by our devotion to justice, and objective as only an ecumenical fellowship can be. In part we are right in this, though in more modest terms. The ecumenical fellowship does have a possibility of seeing things in a universal perspective which is not so accessible to peoples and governments taken one by one. It is not, at least to the same extent, pressed upon by strong vested interests. It ought to be freer to tell the truth and to think in world terms. But we have to know ourselves too, and our ecclesiastical institutions. These also are vested interests.

The survival of the church itself in a hostile environment in a particular country or culture may seem to depend on all of us being a little careful what we say politically out loud. On the other hand, we may calculate that unless we espouse enthusiastically a 'progressive' movement, however ambiguous, the future position of the church in that region will be seriously prejudiced. We are not completely objective. We, too, have vested interests, albeit ecclesiastical ones. One suspicion in past centuries has been that the political church could not resist the temptation to use its power to serve its own advancement (often because that seemed important in the service of the gospel) rather than to defend the cause of mankind. How can we be sure that this is no longer the case?

How then can we see the power of the church properly exercised in the political field? The answer beginning to suggest itself is that we have to be thoroughly non-conformist in our conception of power in this context. 'How many divisions has the Pope?' Stalin is believed to have remarked derisively, but perfectly correctly. Other men in authority have questioned resolute church deputations, asking them what body of electors they truly represented. The answer has to be that this is not the power the church can wield, practically or properly. And as we delve into the problem we are faced with the essential gospel weakness of the church, reflecting as it does, the weakness of God. For we may assume that whatever political pressures the church can mount efficiently, they are as nothing to the pressures which the Creator of all things could exercise had He a mind to do so. But He apparently has not. Nor should we. This is one of the most unwelcome elements of non-conformity Christians have to learn in an age of activism, power and secularity.

Fundamentally the job of the church is to witness, not to compel. That is why it is an essentially peculiar and non-conformist element in the political world. In the world of politics, the effective units are the pressure groups, however discreetly their pressure is applied, however much the power to influence is latent and tacit. Often the church would like to see itself as such a pressure group, getting things done, exerting real power. And sometimes the ecumenical movement is welcomed precisely because it could augment that real power. 'Just think what we could do in the world, if only all of us Christians spoke with a single voice?' But we must remember that such a possibility would rightly fill the hearts of a lot of other men with resentment and foreboding. What reason have they to think we would use such power wisely? None, if history is any guide.

On the contrary, we are much more likely to use it to absolutize the relativities of politics, to enhance conflict to the level of religious wars, to destroy the tolerance of opposing opinions on which political solutions depend, and to give undue primacy to the interest of ecclesiastical institutions. And that is a pretty formidable threat, when all is added up, to the peace of mind of the human race, but one which history does not allow us to gainsay.

So let us abjure political power for the church once and for all. Even if the fashion of our day is to regard such total abstinence as feeble, cowardly and ineffective, let us be non-conformist enough to judge ourselves by our own standards, and not be brow-beaten into adopting categories of judgement which have no particular Christian validity. The function of the church is to be and to witness, not to rule. When it tries to do other people's jobs it makes an ungodly mess of them. When it sticks to its own, it discovers even with surprise that it can be useful rather than dominant. And that, after all, is in accordance with the rôle of its Lord who washed people's feet.

It is going to require a very forceful type of non-conformity to sustain this position. In so far as there may be any moral prestige still adhering to the Christian church, in the minds of men in general, then they will covet the support of the church for policies they passionately believe to be the right ones. They will expect the church to come off the fence, to denounce their opponents, to identify itself with their cause, to put the whole weight of its support behind what they conceive to be morally commendable, and ultimately to become a significant agent of political influence.

Men will not see, in the heat of the struggle, what kind of djinn they are letting out of the bottle. For, in the short run, they are glad of any allies they can get, and resentful of any who refuse allegiance. Nor can they be expected to understand the peculiar self-understanding of the Christian church. It is not a club of those who share a political judgement—far from it. Its very nature is to welcome those who are at odds with the society of their time, those who cannot easily get on together. For they are the essential sign that this is no partisan fellowship but the promise and foretaste of a human family from which none is excluded. And none means none—right wing as well as left wing, white as well as black, poor as well as rich, the lot. Not that they will or can retain their arrogance and pride within such a family, and those who try to do so will exclude themselves. But it does mean that the church cannot identify itself in any simple way with political programmes, without adopting a totally new and unwarranted test of membership for itself.

So, if the church may neither identify simply with other people's political programmes nor exert effective political power itself, what is left to it? The answer is to be found in a fresh understanding of two apparently dusty ideas—spiritual authority and witness to a good which is out of this world. The reason why these two ideas are due for a revival is that they answer to the demand of our time for a new integrity and a new basis for criticism of our society. 'Tell it like it really is', the demand to be told the truth which exercises its own authority over our minds and spirits and is free from suggestions and adaptations designed to conform us to the purposes of others—the whole reaction against the world of advertisement and public relations techniques—this is basically a demand for new recognition of the primacy of spiritual authority. And secondly, the search for a larger, deeper good than the accepted norms of existing societies is a new assertion of non-conformity to which the church supremely can and should respond. Both elements are of such importance that they deserve a paragraph apiece.

'Spiritual authority' can be misused to mean the supremacy of the ecclesiastical authorities. This is precisely not what is intended here. What we are after is a definition of the power which the church can properly exercise over the minds and spirits of men. The essence of spiritual authority is its capacity to evoke the free response of other spirits, to hold up before them something which they freely recognize as good, valuable, great, humane, true— something which, by its own quality, evokes allegiance, respect, reverence, commitment. Of course we are free to reject what is good and true, and that is the limitation of spiritual authority. It has no second line of defence, except to bear the consequences of rejection, and to go on displaying the good that is rejected. It has to resist all the temptations to call in other kinds of power to compel acceptance. Threats of painful or inconvenient consequences, attempts to get behind the rationality of others to their hidden psychological fears and appetites and to play on these to secure allegiance—these are the betrayals of spiritual authority.

The church has no other weapon than the truth of the gospel and its capacity to win response from free men; and whenever it is tempted to reach for something a bit more 'practical' it destroys its own peculiar rôle. There is an inbuilt 'ineffectiveness' here which we must accept, if we are to be true to Christian non-conformity. The power of the church in the field of world politics consists simply in the self-authenticating truth of that to which it faithfully bears witness. It has no other power and it should not want any.

And secondly, the truth to which it bears witness is out of this world. By this is meant—not an other-worldly irrelevance—but something which is always a future possibility, beyond any immediate political programme. The immediate, the relative, the ambiguous choices of the present are controlled by that future, but they have not the same clarity and integrity. The good to which the church points actually calls into question all the possibilities of the moment. None are perfect, but some are more hopeful than others. We have to share in the struggle to decide which of the present ambiguous possibilities is most likely to bring us nearer that which is out-of-this-world good. But equally we have to resist all the pressures to identify this or that political programme with the good which we are called to proclaim.

An illustration may perhaps make these points clearer. Take, for instance, the burning issue of race, the relation of communities of different colours tied together in one geographical and economic complex in such places as southern Africa. Now it is clear that the church, the foretaste of the human family, can have no place for first and second class citizens. The truth, and the good to which it is called to bear witness, is of a community which knows nothing of Jew and Gentile, Greek and barbarian, male and female, as ultimate and inbuilt divisions between human beings. These distinctions—and they are in one sense perfectly real—cannot be used to support privileged positions or to permit one group to lord it by rights over another.

All practical policies have to be controlled by that over-riding truth to which the Church is committed. Moreover, when a ruling class tries to justify a policy of discrimination in elevated pseudo-theological terms, the church has 'to tell it like it really is'—to keep on pointing to the economic exploitation, human injustice, and social deprivation lying behind high sounding political philosophies. In this witness it exercises its proper power. Even more costly, it has to expose the latent violence of an oppressive régime which imposes its will on men through the 'respectable' processes of legality. This will ensure that it avoids some kind of Christian approval reserved only for policies of non-violence. In a violent struggle either both sides repent or neither does.

But it keeps in mind always the goal and the good to which it is committed—a family of mankind in which colour brings enrichment and variety, not estrangement and oppression. Whatever be the debatable immediate options they are tested by that criteria. Is it necessary to separate two communities before they can learn to live together decently? Can it be done in practice, with tolerable fairness? Can the privileged be persuaded to concede anything till they begin to feel the challenge of real countervailing power? How can such power be exercised to achieve an eventual harmony rather than a simple reversal of injustice?

These are questions to which the church as such can give no special answer, of peculiar authority. It can and must participate in the debate, for otherwise the truth it is there to serve remains remote, in the clouds. But it is no more committed to a policy of violence or non-violence in principle, to separation or integration as an immediate device, than it is to a world monetary system based on gold. It has simply to ask—does this proceed from a fundamental contempt or fear of fellow men, does it aim at reconciliation or estrangement, will it perpetuate injustice or tend to create new opportunities for overcoming it.

The answer is never certain, never perfect, never within the competence of the church itself, and certainly never one to which the church can or should lend political power within its reach. Its authority remains spiritual authority alone, its truth lies beyond the range of immediate achievement, yet it is inextricably linked with the political possibilities of today.

5 Politics and Propaganda

The power of the church's witness in international politics resides exclusively in its self-authenticating truth—that was the argument of the last chapter.

We have no other weapon than truth, and we ought not to cast around for any other. For any other method of winning friends and influencing people is contradictory both to the church's own nature and to the gospel committed to us. Christian pacifism is a persistent attempt to project this fundamental and essential Christian principle, valid for the Church's life, on to the plane of world politics in too simple a way. But never let it be forgotten that even by such an exaggeration it has put the whole church in its debt. For the Christian pacifist constantly challenges the church to resist playing politics according to the world's rules. We are reminded that the church's victory can only be a spiritual victory, a winning over of the free unprejudiced spiritual allegiance of other men, a victory without the use of force, physical or psychological, overt or by subtle suggestion. It must be a victory which truth wins unaided.

That is very easy to say, and many people will assent to it until it comes to the crunch. It is likely to prove the major and bloodiest battle ground of the church in this field in the years ahead. So we must understand in greater detail what is implied and what is required for faithfulness in this respect. But to encourage us in this task it is exciting to contemplate how it corresponds with some of the deepest and most courageous acts of non-conformity which we witness today.

The crowds demonstrating in Prague in 1968 were chanting the old cry of Czechoslovak dissent—'Tell us the truth'. They feared that they were going to be wrapped once again in the misty cobwebs of ideological propaganda, their minds intoxicated by inaccurate information, their capacity for judgement thereby stolen. But were they saying in principle anything more radical than the students on American campuses calling in chorus 'Tell it like it really is'? They too feel suffocated by a consensus propaganda of a whole society which presents a roseate, sugary and optimistic account of an essentially unjust and inhuman situation. They cry for non-conformity, for the courage to stand up before the majority and the powerful and restore integrity to language again—calling a spade a spade for a change. In part they are in revolt against a world of propaganda, designed to put us into a state of comfortable anaesthesia, the one-dimensional society of Herbert Marcuse.

'Tell it like it really is'—'Tell us the truth'—these are cries which the church must hear. But let there be no false optimism about the church's response. The likelihood is that it will fail, and the most likely people to betray it may well be the radicals within the church. This startling possibility must be examined.

'Truth—what is it? It is a bourgeois concept.' So one of the leaders of the African Liberation movements is reported to maintain. The man of action, whatever his political philosophy, will always tend to despise the academic, contemplative, 'objective' service of truth. 'Truth' for him is not something static, unchanging, transcendent but a weapon to be used in conflict. He is not so interested in simply understanding the world—he wants, like Marx, to change it. And he lays hold of 'truth' as a tool for his use.

The illustration from Africa may suggest that this attitude to truth is in some way peculiar to the anti-bourgeois left. So let us balance it on the right. Henry Faerlie recounts the following anecdote of Winston Churchill:

'When Churchill was in opposition after 1945, he led the Conservative Party in a debate about the Health Service. As he listened to Aneurin Bevan's opening speech, he called for some statistics about the rate of infant mortality in recent years to use in his reply; they were supplied, copiously and accurately, by Iain Macleod, then working in the back rooms of the Conservative Research Department. But, in his speech, Churchill made only one bold and sweeping use of the detailed figures which he had been given and, in the corridors afterwards, stopped Macleod: "I gather, young man, that you wish to be a Member of Parliament. The first lesson that you must learn is that, when I call for statistics about the rate of infant mortality, what I want is proof that fewer babies died when I was Prime Minister than when anyone else was Prime Minister. That is a political statistic." '

Before we get horrified by what appears to be the fanaticism of the left or the cynicism of the right, we should pause to reflect. Men who want to change things are not by any means morally worse than those who want to describe things as they are. To change things you need power, and one element of power is the capacity to persuade other men. If some over-simplification is necessary to do this on a grand scale, then so be it. The alternative is an endless process of intricate discussion and dialogue which will evade decisiveness. We shall all, like Hamlet, be 'sicklied o'er with the pale cast of thought', and nothing will get done.

Today men call for action. The more radical and non-conformist we are, the more we yearn for real, reforming, revolutionary action which will do a fundamental job of altering the human condition. Action is all, because we are so deeply dissatisfied with the *status quo*. But action, the use of power to change things, is, as we have seen, a potential enemy of truth. Never mind whether a thing is true or not—will it produce the sort of response we want, the sort of action we consider desirable?

All of this is further magnified by the burgeoning influence of the mass media. An engineer, for instance, may discuss with a journalist in relative detachment whether a particular type of system-building of tall blocks of flats will safely withstand certain wind pressures. Put the same man on television one evening, after the collapse of such a building, and let him say the same things, and the effect can be stunning or electrifying on thousands of families instantly. Should he be allowed or prevented? If he is speaking the strict truth, is it a proper question to ask what the likely effect will be on the peace of mind of many without available alternative accommodation? Or must truth be served, on television, at any cost? We are driven to conclude that 'truth is a bourgeois concept' if it is detached from all its social consequences.

We can now begin to see why the betrayal of the truth is most likely to come from men of goodwill deeply committed to action to change things, be they in the church or outside it. To get a whole society on the move requires a mood of crusade rather than one of discussion and debate. The critic and the questioner should be discouraged. The general good requires an end to awkward disputations. And we end with the strange but familiar phenomenon—that the dissenting social idealist rapidly becomes the man most impatient of criticism, the enemy of freedom of thought.

Here once again we recognize the rôle of the church as the most relentless non-conformist of them all. And we can see why. The testimony of the church is always to a society which is not attainable in history, to a reality which on earth will always be seen in a glass darkly. Every political crusade is assessed for what it is—neither as ultimate nor as perfect as its devoted promoters would contend, nor as diabolical and destructive as its enemies accuse it of being. When all men are shouting in terms of black and white, the church ought to know better, and, unpopular with both sides, keep stressing the shades of grey. This is not because of some desire for detachment or wish to evade the issue. Far from it. For with this discernment of ambiguity in our human political affairs, there must also go a demand and a challenge that people should have the courage to discriminate heroically, as best they can, between the shades of grey.

We have to realize what we are up against. Nowadays the parties to an international conflict give high priority to the propaganda weapon. Immense resources and highly sophisticated ingenuity go into building up an image of oneself as innocent, helpless, humane, wronged before the eyes of the world. Then modern mass communications are available to project this image into everyone's home. Moreover, the competition for attention between newspapers, radio and television channels provokes each to seek a dramatic and striking presentation—which is far easier to achieve if you can use stark blacks and whites than if you are compelled by old fashioned honesty to mix the two a bit. To anyone whose knowledge of affairs has to be of a less superficial nature there is something agonizing in watching the process at work—particularly when it is specifically and intentionally aimed at church people and 'men of goodwill'.

How readily they fall victims, for the best and most generous reasons. Yet how much better it would be if their heads were a little harder than their hearts. The achievements of propaganda in oversimplifying one issue after another—Vietnam, Middle East, Nigeria and Biafra—were matched only by the readiness of church people to be fed with this kind of tale in categories belonging to the stage of cowboys and Indians. Such categories provide a release of the moral judgement, even if at the same time they offer an escape from the real world, with all its agonizing bewilderment and living by faith.

I have warned that today those likely to betray the truth may well be the radical activists. It must be added that now and always, and for other particular reasons, a similar temptation haunts the church. For the religious community inescapably draws to itself, among many types of men and women, those who are drawn to the church because they find reality itself particularly hard to bear. T. S. Eliot remarked that men cannot tolerate much reality, and every doctor, psychiatrist, and pastor would assent. Religion certainly cannot be dismissed simply as an opiate of the people, but Charles Kingsley was right at least in suggesting that many people prefer it to drugs or other forms of escape to fulfil the purpose. That being so, it is peculiarly difficult for a Christian community to live with the harsh realities of international anarchy and the fearful threats to human survival implicit in that anarchy today.

There was a vivid example of the condition at the Fourth Assembly of the World Council of Churches in 1968. A film was shown, of a documentary nature, slightly out of date, the commentary in North American English, depicting coolly but horribly the arms confrontation in the world, the sabre rattling of the two great super powers, the spread of weapons elsewhere. At once a sharp reaction was set up among the viewers. No one questioned the facts as presented, the nature and number of weapons, their potential threat. But many felt that somehow the element of conflict and confrontation could be abated if we pretended that the situation was less terrible. The longing for detente involved a preference for attending to less unpleasant realities. Four weeks later the aeroplanes we had seen on the screen were landing on the airport at Prague or resuming their pulverizing missions in North Vietnam. Could we not bear the truth—the very people whose faith centres on a crucifixion? 'Could you not watch with me one hour?'

This perhaps leads us to the heart of the matter. To face the truth is to accept the ministry of suffering—and it is much more agreeable to be activists. If we are putting the world right we can feel pretty good. If we 'tell it as it really is' we must also be prepared to feel pretty bad, weeping with those who weep, acknowledging the human condition as surely Christians, of all people, ought to recognize it. But we betray the young, and please God they know it, every time we pretend that kind words and sweet thoughts are a proper substitute for facing things as they really are. We shall not learn what love is until we learn something of its helplessness and its suffering.

Such a rôle for the church implies several things. It requires, for instance, its own professional organ to make an independent, 'non-conformist' judgement on the affairs of the day. Of course such an agency will lean heavily on the work of kindred bodies, universities and institutes, dedicated to objective research and assessment too. Equally certainly, it will never be 'popular' in the accepted sense. For the clamour of the day will always demand partisanship and commitment to human causes far beyond what they can properly command in Christian terms. So anyone who thinks the operation could be usefully developed as an aspect of the church's public relations is bound for disappointment. Perhaps it is just as well, for that kind of double think cuts at the root of the main thing the church can properly contribute—a devotion to the truth for its own sake, not as a means to achieve reflected glory oneself.

6 Standing for Righteousness

The scene is the site of the Fourth Assembly of the World Council of Churches in Uppsala, Sweden. Outside the great Sports Hall the wide steps and pavement are occupied by the unlikely scattering of people that adorn such events—Swedish police, television and press photographers, ecclesiastics in every kind of uniform, even Ian Paisley rather forlornly walking up and down unnoticed in a white inscribed waistcoat. In such company it is hard to make a startling impression.

Inside the hall the weary delegates, in a heavy atmosphere of much used air, are labouring to conclude the final debate on international affairs—what should the Assembly advise on Vietnam, the Middle East, Nigeria? As the meeting disperses through every door I see a distinguished diplomat, known and loved for his sensitive Christian humanity, striding angrily down the steps, his face in a fierce frown. 'No different from the UN' he complains, 'only more irresponsible. If I thought there was the least chance of the President of the USA heeding that advice, I would regard it as my solemn duty to humanity to assassinate him forthwith'. Then broodingly he adds, 'why do we so easily become organized Pharisees?'

I repeat the tale because this book is about non-conformity; his was a good example. It is particularly difficult to open one's ears to the non-conformist at the end of a long laborious conference when one is at last in sight of the closing session, and wearily anxious for reassurance that one's labours have not been in vain. But there is no escape. For it is precisely at the moment when everyone present is emotionally eager to be patted on the back, and so is peculiarly susceptible to self-delusion, that the astringent voice of questioning is most required to keep us in touch with reality. Yet the last question of the speaker is the one that haunts the mind, whenever one reflects on the Christian rôle in international affairs. Are we just being Pharisees in a big way?

The case for the prosecution is formidable enough. For we naturally start from the assumption that if there is one thing the Church should be good at it is distinguishing right from wrong. After all, are we not in some way the guardians of the moral law? We may not be politically very adept or experienced. We may have to admit (a little reluctantly perhaps) that the men who run foreign ministries and all the paraphernalia of government—or opposition for that matter—may have knowledge and skills we cannot ourselves aspire to. But, lest thereby they escape our critical judgement, we hasten to add that experts can be fools at the same time—and then we play our trump card; in some sense we are the people who know about right and wrong better than they do.

And that is, one supposes, precisely what the Pharisees thanked God for too. They were not, after all, as other men, a fact for which they had every reason to be grateful. They were certainly not as these sinners, these manipulators of power, these compromisers and calculators, these men who put party before principle, these politicians so blinded by their obsession with immediate advantages that they cannot see beyond their own noses. Thank God for us, the Christians—surely we must in duty bound give the lost world the benefit of our insights?

Put that way, we can already detect a false note somewhere. But we do not need to put it that way. We can say instead that it is our function to deal with 'moral issues' rather than political technicalities. Then we are certainly back in what seems a familiar main stream Christian tradition. But in fact we have simply confused the issue with high sounding words. For 'moral' is defined as referring to the difference between right and wrong. Certainly every decision under the sun is one which involves a choice—and every choosing is an attempt to select the right from the wrong, whether it is done by a churchman or an atheist. We can get very confused in a peculiarly Anglo-Saxon way on this point, imagining that if we pronounce the word 'moral' with enough solemnity we have lifted the debate on to a higher plane.

Lord Grey, when he was Foreign Secretary, is credited with the portentous rumination: 'To do the right thing is, generally speaking, the right thing to do.' His words at least hint at the underlying problem, especially by his use of the cautious qualification 'generally speaking'. For he thus suggests that it is not so simply possible to disentangle morals and technicalities—that our choices are not limitless, bounded only by our hopes and dreams and imaginings, but are in large measure defined by circumstances. The real problem is to judge accurately what the real alternatives are in a given situation—a faculty which is partly expertise, partly art and experience, and partly hope and imagination—and then to select the alternative which appears to maximize the good possibilities.

Here, surely, is where the gospel intervenes—in one's judgement of which possibilities are 'good'. And our criteria here are not moral rules in a legal sense but our gradually dawning sense of what the Bible and Christian tradition tells us God is like.

The booby-traps awaiting us on this path are two-fold. The first is that it *does* require a mixture of expertise, art and experience to discern the very alternatives between which we must choose. And all too often the churchmen who want to do the choosing lack these particular gifts. After all they are neither universal nor are they conveyed by baptism or a theological education. If one is to look anywhere for them, one would try first the circles of those people who are actually on the job—and they are usually too busy to attend church gatherings.

That is one trap—that we talk in the absence of those best fitted to help us. But, secondly, we can overlook the fact that many a man engaged in politics is using criteria of good and evil, right and wrong as efficiently as we can hope to do. If his theology is woolly or non-existent, his wrestling with reality is perhaps more candid and courageous, and the net result may be a considerable improvement on our own performance.

Now we can begin to see a little daylight. If we perceive, from the start and really radically, that Christians and the Churches are *not* the guardians of the moral order, that the light which lighteth every man coming into the world often shines more brightly outside the church than in it, we suddenly discover an escape from Pharisaism. We are not in the world to put everyone else right, to lecture the naughty world on its bad behaviour, to issue statements to the powers of the world expressing our general indignation with respect to their evil habits. That would be (and often, alas, is) pure Pharisaism.

We are instead called to engage in the life of a world where men are often much better than we are, as well as being also more diabolical than our sentimentalizing expects. We are called to go out and find our allies, of every faith and no formal faith at all, and to get stuck in alongside such people, offering such contributions as we may possess without any pretensions. And through it all, we are expected to preach 'not ourselves, but Christ crucified'. Instead of taking it upon ourselves to be the moral members of mankind, our job is simply to point, and keep on pointing, to the one who is our own judge as well as the world's—and, in the light of our own preaching, to join the human race in its struggle for justice and order.

The Pharisaic temptation is to join nothing which is less pure than we conceive ourselves to be—to stand a little apart, above the complexities and technicalities and calculations which 'ordinary' men wrestle with, to strive for a position from which, with immense superiority, we can pronounce the simple moral truth that everyone else ignores. The great thing is that this does a world of good to our own anxious ecclesiastical egos—specially at a time when they are otherwise in some distress. For it puts us in some way on top—we are the judges of the world. Nor should we be surprised by our own temerity. We are in good company. Was this not precisely the ambition of those two intimate disciples, James and John, whom we revere?

When Jesus had made that heady promise that in the last days the disciples would have thrones of their own and judge at least the twelve tribes of Israel, if not the rest of the human race, the seeds of ambition were sown. Might not James and John aspire to being the chiefest judges of all, one on the right hand and the other on the left hand of the king himself? The answer was apparently solemn and reflective about the fact that they could scarcely be expected to realize what they were talking about. For positions like that are reserved for those who at the same time lay down their lives for mankind, not simply for those attending solemn assemblies. 'Can you drink the cup that I drink?' It is attractive to be a judge, but totally expensive to be a saviour. For the Christian, however, it is clear that he who aspires to be the first must be prepared for the cost of the second. That is the recollection which properly silences our wordiness when we set out to tell the world how to be moral, and vote ourselves the prophets' mantle without taking up his cross.

Perhaps, therefore, we do well to suspect ourselves when we begin to behave as though we were enthroned above the troubles of mankind, handing down judgements on men's conflicts. Who in heaven's name are we who take this upon ourselves? While we remain denominations even we can often see through our folly. But an ecumenical throne is another matter—it has just sufficient grandeur in the sight of men to deceive us into settling comfortably into it, and from it conferring on our fellows the benefit of our moral advice.

So if we want to be true Christian non-conformists we need a totally different image of ourselves to live up to. The one that springs to mind, as the best prophylactic against Pharisaism, is the image of Jesus washing the feet of troubled men. If lords and kings we wish to be, in the non-conforming kingdom, what better eccentricity than that of being a foot-washing community? There can be no pretensions about that. It means joining the human race and being really involved in its needs, which are our own. At last the dichotomy between moral principle and technical possibility begins to fade away, for the man who is set on *doing* something for his neighbour—not just talking at him—will feel a tremendous moral obligation to get down to the technicalities with him to find out what is the best thing to do. And in doing so he will discover that often he has to learn from his neighbour about these very technicalities, has to sit at his feet to be taught as well as to wash them.

The picture that emerges from all this is itself instructive. We are doing our job best, not when we are on our own in the great assemblies of our ecclesiastical and ecumenical institutions, calling out across a gulf to the tortured, struggling world beyond. Rather, we are really in the right place only when we are in the company of all the other publicans and sinners (like ourselves), talking with them, planning with them, learning from them, and all the time in living awareness of Him who is the only judge of us all, and who is equally the saviour of us all. The publicans and sinners may, in this context, be men of power and authority. Equally they may be the wretched of the earth, the underground, the dissenters and leaders of revolutionary movements. Our test is not the world's test—we do business with any man who takes seriously the welfare of mankind. And we learn from them, even before we start teaching ourselves.

Certainly this is non-conformist—if we think for a moment of the 'normal' way we and our churches go about our work in this field. But it is a non-conformity which offers new prospects and new methods of escaping from the occupational disease of the religious spirit—the disease of Pharisaism.

7 Opiate of the People

It was, of course, Charles Kingsley rather than Karl Marx who coined the phrase about religion being the opiate of the people. I register this familiar fact simply to claim the idea itself as a splendid and valuable example of Christian nonconformity in politics. Kingsley was telling the truth, not simply for Victorian England of the industrial revolution, but for all times and ages. He was pointing to a tendency in all religious people which we never completely resist, and which forever bedevils the work which Christians and churches attempt in international affairs. It is the tendency to believe in fairies. It is the longing to picture for ourselves a world which is nicer, more comfortable, less appalling than the one which we walk into on Monday morning. And it is the use made of religion to justify these fantasies of ours.

We can rationalize this procedure in all kinds of subtle ways. For example, we can say that religion and the church stands for the ideal over against those hard faced men of power who are 'realists'. This allows us to fly away to our dream world of beauty and delight, leaving someone else to clear up the actual mess in which men presently find themselves. But it does worse than that. It makes God himself part of a never-never land, not someone we are likely to meet today when we are deciding how to vote, whether to protest, what to do with our money. God becomes part of an ideal world, and evidently this is not an ideal world. So the church takes up a position several thousand feet above the mêlée, and shouts down to the people below a mixture of condemnation and impossible exhortations regarding their behaviour, advocating conduct only possible for those who have their feet no longer on the ground.

Obviously such an attitude is silly and irrelevant, but it is also more sinister than that. Churches which pursue this sort of 'idealism' in public affairs have thereby an infinite capacity to fool themselves about their own involvement, as institutions, and as social groups, in the real tough mêlée on earth. When the going gets rough, when oppressed and under privileged groups are no longer content to observe the 'civilized courtesies', when men really confront one another with their opposing interests, when nations are embattled, when crude power is being exercised overtly or covertly, the idealist religious man finds himself faced with a reality far beyond what he can cope with. He begins to crank up his spiritual helicopter and take to the skies, so as to escape the real battle. At that point religion can be an opiate indeed.

So we are brought sharply into the debate between the idealists and the realists, and up against the question of the proper posture of the church in this respect. And we had better recognize, at the outset, that churches which are largely middle class suburban, reflecting a reasonably contented segment of the community, will always tend in the direction of an idealistic, liberal, kindly, but sentimental attitude to the world's problems. Desperation, agony, terror, bitter resentment—these are not common experiences in such societies. People can easily believe that a tolerable harmony is readily available if only everyone would be a bit more neighbourly and thoughtful. The experience of two starving people before a scrap of food enough to keep one only alive is not familiar. But of course this is the experience that provokes 'realism', and it is the way in which life comes to the majority of mankind. If student protest and 'hippie' extravagances can break through the cosy cocoon of our 'normal' world, and reveal to us how utterly abnormal it is, perhaps we may yet be saved. But, like the camel going through the eye of a needle, it is not easy to envisage how it can happen to people like us.

Realism about what life on earth is really like for most people—that is one thing. But there must also be realism about how it works. Perhaps the opiate works here with almost equal viciousness. We want to envisage a world in which we are free to pursue our lives without interfering or being interfered with. It is of course a dream. We refuse to recognize that to live is to exert power, to create is to control others, to be (quite simply) is to limit the possibilities of other beings. So we are for ever chasing the chimera of a human society in which the distasteful elements of power, of imposed patterns, and structures of human limitations, no longer exist. One formulation of this notion is 'General and Complete Disarmament'. Of course it would be nice to live in a world where that is a conceivable achievement. No one questions its desirability any more than one questions the desirability of a world government which is at the same time non-tyrannical. The question is its attainability—or rather, even more serious, whether in the process of trying to attain it we shall not in fact create a situation far more dangerous than the one we aim to remedy. Here we simply cannot afford *not* to be realists, in the sense of taking account of evidence and experience.

The argument is pulling us however reluctantly in the direction of the 'realists', those hard men who actually do political things, rather than write or preach about them. They are found in respectable Whitehall offices, and in cheap basement flats—running the official machine or tuning up the underground resistance. But they have in common a keen interest in finding out how societies work and how they can be made to work differently. Woe betide us in the churches if we think we can act or speak relevantly in the field of international politics without letting them teach us what they know.

Having said so much in which I profoundly believe, I would not want what follows to detract one fraction of it. Yet plain honesty requires one to add a word about a feature of our present day youthful protest. In the name of realism, and by way of a radical criticism of so much accepted liberal sentimentality, we are now offered a panacea of revolution which returns us to fantasy by another route. In a curious way, liberal optimism is seen out through the front door and smuggled in again through the back. Once again an attempt is made to restore the illusion that a world of harmony is waiting to be won. The only difference is that the means required are more apocalyptic and less reformist. And once again men and women side-step the real questions of power and organization and conflicting wills and human pride and dreams of glory.

Let us be clear—the choice between reformist policies and revolutionary ones is a pragmatic one, and a Christian realist, in the sense we have commended, has no *a priori* preference for one over the other. Which will bring justice to men with the least suffering for them? Which will open up the future with the greatest promise? Will the destructive consequences of revolution outweigh the

advantages of bringing quickly to an end an intolerable situation?
And have you the forces to win, one way or the other? The element
of fantasy enters at the point of romantic enthusiasm where such
calculations are no longer reckoned out, and where revolution for
its own sake is embraced wildly, excitedly, irrationally, as much a
reaction of frustration and despair as a pursuit of human welfare.
However, such policies are advertised as examples of new found
realism, they are really the same old fantasies as father indulged
in, only attired in a more bizarre uniform.

'All fantasy works like a drug—whether it takes the form of
addiction to power or sex or television or revolutionary politics, it
is all progressively addictive, demands increasing gratification and
ends, however subtly, in one form or another of frustration.'

Like all wild generalizations that statement contains a sufficient
grain of truth to put us on our guard. But it reminds us too that
what we are seeking in our Christian faith is an escape from fantasy,
a coming-to-terms with reality. That alone is salvation and therein
alone is hope that creativity will take the place of frustration.

The writer goes on: 'Ultimately all fantasy is a form of sickness
or madness—whether temporary or lasting, a disturbance of our
mental equilibrium with the reality of the world around us.'

One can see the sober 'realist' rubbing his hands complacently
together as he reads these words. So, in order to offer him a last
word of Christian non-conformity, something more has to be said.
For the truth is that Christians see reality not only as (but certainly
including) the daily visible earthly world that hits us week after
week. This is the aspect of reality which we have to learn about and understand if we are ever to be able to manipulate it, divert it, control it.
But it is the only reality the so-called 'realists' ever attend to. For
us there is a larger reality, encompassing rather than contradicting
what we see with our eyes—a reality we cannot actually see but
which captures our faith and allegiance in Jesus Christ. There is no
mystical escape here from the brutalities, cruelties and alienations of
history, for Jesus is not simply a fine example, He is a crucified
person. His fate and His triumph encompass and contain all the
realisms of our hard world without denying them or giving us any
excuse, in the name of idealism, for ignoring them. But He discloses
that of themselves they are not the whole story by any means.

That is why the realistic posture of the Church in politics can be,
at one and the same time, unblinkingly frank, unshockable, never

offended by the necessities of political calculation—and also, in witness to its Lord who is the most real reality of all, straining towards unknown futures which miraculously transcend anything a purely worldly mind can conceive. For the church there are always more possibilities in an international situation than the idle or the disillusioned cynic will recognize, but there is also a more disciplined and cross-bearing acceptance of earthly means and limitations than the idealist has courage to allow. If that means a two-sided non-conformity, we must not complain.

8 Logic and Insight

If one finds oneself in a common-room of young doctors, it is perfectly possible to be shocked by the conversation. Do these men have no feeling for the humiliations to which we are subject? Are they blind to the fact that it is persons they are dealing with, not simply interesting conditions? Often we have the same reaction when we overhear the normal language used between each other by professionals in the field of politics. It is even more striking among soldiers and defence experts. There is, no doubt, a logic and a rationality in what they are saying. But the underlying mood and sentiment seems to have a crazy inhumanity about it which renders the whole conversation grotesquely bizarre.

No doubt we are right up to a point. We can respect much of the youth protest which calls in question the 'scientific logic' which gives us marvellous multiple warhead missiles, independently targeted as they burst into the atmosphere from outer space, but leaves us with inadequate housing in the interval before doomsday. If this is 'reason' then let us have some passionate lunacy. The horrid world that scientific and technological wisdom seems to promise, which offers everything except what our humanity and our art depend upon—motorways to replace our gardens, space travel to soothe our alienation from each other, computerized decision-making to spare us the elation of personal commitment in faith— is not this the greatest enemy against everything the church should stand for?

Compassion, humanity, the capacity to feel for one another again —are not these far more important than all the scientific arguments and sophisticated political analyses and skills upon which 'the establishment' so blindly relies?

It is a dull soul who has never entertained these questions, and it is more than time that he should begin to do so. What reason and logic is it that presents us enthusiastically with more and more of what we don't want, and leaves us starving and afraid for the things which mean most to us? In our despair many people today seek escape from reason itself, into emotional commitment, and aesthetic sensibility. 'Normally this would be a problem for the culture alone. But there are crucial sociological problems as well. For the new style in culture spills over into politics and seeks to justify the destruction of civility and discourse. At its most extreme, it seeks to justify aesthetics, it becomes a justification of the gesture, and of the extreme act.' We recognize at once the familiar scene of public protest, with its almost desperate search for integrity, and its fierce rejection of 'civility'.

Now this is the world we shall live in for the rest of the century. So it is important for the church to take its bearings in it, and decide what the style of its activity should be in relation to these sweeping storms of the human spirit. It will not surprise those who appreciate my fundamental commitment to Christian non-conformity that I for one refuse either to embrace or to reject this tendency to anti-reason in international affairs. There will be tremendous pressures and temptations to prove to oneself, even if to no one else, that the Christian faith and the church has a future in the public life of men, by showing how readily it identifies itself with the new tides of human sensibility. But such an uncritical allegiance, as we shall see, spells disaster. And it is bound to create its own backlash in the minds of sober men and women who will be driven to an exaggerated defence of traditional establishments and systems of reasons and logic by the very excesses of their wilder critics.

Why cannot we say that the rôle of the church today is simply to restore 'the heart' to politics, and to call in question 'the head'?

Let us go back to the medical common-room. Amongst the young men so apparently irresponsibly and flippantly tossing around medical anecdotes, some will probably achieve a life's work of healing and relief of suffering that would be the envy of the softest hearted. They will do this not simply by the quality of their sympathy but equally, or even more, by their determination to understand why certain conditions arise and what is effective in treating them. A disciplined, detached, clinical mind may be far more important to the patient than sympathy devoid of knowledge. 'If I fell into a river,' said that truly compassionate Archbishop, William Temple, 'I would be more anxious to see on the bank a thief who could swim than a cathedral canon who could not.' What he tended to assume was that the thief would be decent enough to jump in to rescue some stranger in trouble.

Given that initial impulse of concern and compassion, then the next most important quality is competence—skill that never is a stranger to reason. And if at times men allow themselves to indulge in emotional flippancies—as doctors, politicians or soldiers—for some at least this is merely a necessary disengagement to allow them to get on with their work without the distraction of too harrowing an emotional involvement. On the other hand those who expose their hearts totally to the realities of human life may find soon enough that they are rendering themselves unfit to do anything about it except suffer—a valid vocation but not politically relevant.

These are the dangers we face in a period of such enormous transformations of human society as is now ahead. We shall need men of courageous imagination and sensitivity who can break the moulds of conventional thought and practice and open up novelties for us all that we are often too lethargic to contemplate. But we must escape the impotence of the dreamer who leaves behind him nothing but his unsatisfied dreams. So we shall need, too, the practical builder, always tempted to get so absorbed in the technicalities of his job that he has no time to reflect whether what he is creating really meets the case, but without whom nothing at all gets done.

And where better than in the Christian fellowship shall we find the community of persons, disciplined by humanity and a burning commitment at the same time, where the two types of vocation can meet and really listen to what the other side is saying? For this to happen we must preserve a universe of discourse, as well rational as imaginative, where the civilities are preserved which alone make communication possible. In this sense the church must take its stand, in the excited confrontations of our time, in favour of rationality. Equally it is a pilgrim fellowship, forever on the march towards an end it does not see except in a glass darkly. So it has to refuse imprisonment in a conventional 'rationality', a static acceptance of apparent possibilities that blind it to the perfections which God alone discloses.

There are two services it can thus render to our day and age which may turn out to be peculiarly relevant and exciting. First of all, it can nourish and preserve those human links and confidences and elements of mutual trust without which the visionaries of our day find themselves reduced to warring factions, mutually destructive. For it is the experience of all who are seriously engaged in today's protest movements that all too soon their energies are dissipated in internecine feuds. It has been the mark of the truly great amongst the revolutionary leaders of today that they have managed to combine a vivid vision of a better future with a strong and practical realism, capable of drawing together people of different qualities and aspirations to work for strictly practical ends—and to do it by appeal to the common human inheritance of reason. Some short sharp battles can be won by appeal to the mass enthusiasms of the moment. But to win long wars we need to have recourse to something more solid than the evanescent moods of the crowd. There is a hard discipline here which we can learn only from the men of practical experience. In our own Methodist tradition there is solid ground for such an assertion. We were not called Methodists for nothing.

The second service we can render arises from a very deep seated and bewildering ambiguity in our modern society itself. It has been put in this way: 'We are witnessing an extreme disjunction between our culture and our social structure, the one devoted to apocalyptic attitudes, the other to technocratic decision making. How a society can live at all with such a disjunction is a thorny question for the future.' Indeed it may spell the doom of all our striving, for the gulf may prove too deep to be bridged and the coherence of society itself may well be in jeopardy.

In some sense the Christian can bear to consider such a disaster as conceivably the judgement of God upon a world of false values and idolatrous allegiance. Somehow a new start may have to be made. But he cannot lightly conform his actions to this end. In the process of a general breakdown of social and international ties, immense human suffering would be involved, all the greater because the enormous numerical increase of human beings on earth, all needing to be fed and sheltered, puts a premium on preserving basic elements of organization. Our planet is now too crowded to allow us to revert to the simple self-help of our savage past.

So the human task is to bridge that gap between the humanist and the technocrat, the artist and prophet, on the one hand, and the decision makers of our social machine on the other. Perhaps even more important, we have to bridge the gulf of alienation between those few who live in physical comfort as heirs of modern technology in the affluent suburbs of the world, and the many who distantly aspire to the fruits of modern production while hoping to avoid the depersonalizing consequences it has engendered so far.

There is no simple way out for the church at this time. Many are clamouring for it to take sides in this great debate. It seems natural for it to ally itself with men of feeling and sympathy, and to disassociate itself from all who are involved in trying to make the ramshackle 'system' work which we have inherited from history. But the men of sensibility will be eternally frustrated if they fail to construct a system tolerably better, because they will settle for nothing but the impossible best. And the practical realists will prove themselves monumentally irrelevant, fiddlers while Rome itself is burning, if they cannot hear what the men of vision are telling them about the radical changes which must somehow be brought about, whether by small steps or disconcerting strides, if our crowded planet is to survive.

It is not for the church to say that this reconciliation of aspirations is impossible. Perhaps its most radical and revolutionary message for today is that the Christian fellowship itself is the one place where it must be achieved, on behalf of all mankind.

The Christian church was born in revolutionary times. Perhaps we are nearer today to the feel and atmosphere of those days than at any other moment of church history. It was a time of the breaking down of old structures, the collapse of old faiths, the emergence of strange coteries of people looking for apocalyptic events—and it was the beginning of a new sort of world. What men looked for round the next corner took, perhaps, centuries to come to pass and then in a form they had not anticipated. It was said at that time that the Christian community survived because it outlived, outthought and outdied its contemporaries.

Today we are called indeed to find a new style of living, expressing the joy, the confidence, the humility and love of Christianity in terms of a marvellous strange new world society. We are equally called to 'die daily' to that world, as were our forefathers, at a time when men desperately cling to the notion that it is all they have got or can hope for. Not the least of our duties is to go on outthinking our times, to insist that the Christian faith is not an irrational enthusiasm of those whose heads are as soft as their hearts, but a perception of reality, to which our reason also bears its witness, corrupted as Freud would properly insist along with all the biblical tradition, but not rendered thereby useless. Of course we rationalize our interests—our hopes and appetites and anxieties. But then what other capacities do we possess that are free from similar distortions? And when it comes to communicating with each other, only a limited range of messages are conveyed without the use of language and its attendant rationalities.

Politics is the business of achieving communication and joint action between groups of human beings. International politics, bedevilled by international language problems, is the same, only more difficult. Common understanding is hard enough intrinsically, and we simply make it impossible if we minimize the utility of reasoned argument. Then the conflicts of men become insoluble by any means other than the imposition of the will of the most powerful.

So it is surely a basic Christian concern to defend one of the few means we possess of reconciling human wills and enabling people to work together for commonly agreed ends—the principle of reasoned argument, and the sharing of our best rational thinking together. Whatever may be the excitements ahead, we shall continue to rely for our international community on some people who, in the name of Him whom the Bible calls the Logos of the world, are not afraid to use all their intellectual powers and practical expertise in the service of humanity.